Arrows of Youth

Arrows of Youth

A young man's inspiring journey to

find what lights his soul on fire

VINCENT RUSSELL VAN PATTEN

This book is for my friends and family . . . Love has surrounded me my entire life; love that's never judged, only encouraged me to live with a full heart. I will do everything I can to spread that love.

To my mom Betsy, my dad Vincent, my stepmom Eileen, and my brothers Duke and Jesse: Together, life has been nothing short of an adventure—your guidance, passion, and support have given me the opportunity to seek what lights my soul on fire. I love you all, more than you can ever know.

I am grateful beyond words for each of my friends. We're on this journey together—our paths will ebb and flow—but I'll always be there for you.

I'm deeply thankful for the assistance of my editor, Michael Springer. Your historical and literary expertise has been joyful and invaluable.

To the contemporary thinkers, doers, and creators whose ideas and actions I explore in this book: Thank you, from the bottom of my heart. You've been the pillars on which I've leaned in my pursuit of meaning.

You've given me and the world hope, inspiration, and purpose at a pivotal point in human history. The world is a better place due to each of you.

To the historical figures who fascinate me endlessly: You've helped me understand who I am and where I fit into my modern-day. May you stay forever inspired and curious, wherever you are.

←—◄

CONTENTS

PART TWO

THE PACIFIC NORTHWEST

PART THREE

SUNLIGHT OVER ME

FOREWARD

MY SON VINCENT has proven to me he is quite a writer. When he gave up his real estate job a year ago to pursue his dream, I didn't bat an eye. I knew he was serious; I wanted him to be happy. So he had my blessings. Little did I know he was going to be so good and dive in so quickly. It is clear his passion for writing is his true calling and greatest love.

He surprised me when he casually said he was going to be finishing up his first book in a few months. I thought to myself: *Reading or writing?* Yes, that old joke flashed through my mind. But just for temporary amusement. I knew this was for real; I just couldn't believe it. Well, after reading his first draft, he impressed me greatly. It also inspired me; *I think you'll feel the same.* It's rare to see a young man so curious about life and nature in such an inherent and unaffected way. His writings and poetry opened my mind and deepened my soul. They made

Arrows of Youth

me feel like I was drinking water from a cool well on a hot day. This book also taught me about some incredibly fascinating people and ideas. I revisited powerful material I had touched on before, but hadn't fully appreciated in a long time. This book taught me a lot about my son— *what makes him tick. I learned what makes him excited, happy, sad, and curious.*

Arrows of Youth explores his deepest thoughts while dissecting some of the most profound and famous thinkers in history. He examines their theories and intentions to perfection.

On a side note: In a time where people are disconnecting more and more in this world, Vinny goes out there, takes chances, and connects with strangers in a beautiful way. He does so not because he has to, but because he yearns to. I know this book will make you enjoy your day. It will make you smile and perhaps strike up a conversation with a stranger. You'll appreciate every walk, every breath of cool air in the morning, and every scent of changing seasons a whole lot more.

Personally, this book dared me to be even braver and more adventurous in the future. It has encouraged me to take more chances and to go places I used to fear. I thank my son Vinny and this book for that. I'm so glad he had the courage and insight to follow his path and become the writer he knew he had to be. *Some things you just know.*

Vincent Van Patten Senior
Or, POPS

Arrows of Youth

PART ONE

CALIFORNIA

HALF DOME

Seeking

And he ran and ran
Until there was nowhere left to run.

Under the night sky,
Not a twinkle in the stars
But a twinkle in his eye.

A seeker,
Searching for escape,
But from what, or to what, he is unsure.
Only the path that lies ahead, and a heart that is pure.

A hard road
Is what this seeker may find,
A hard road
Each step strengthens his ever-searching mind;

What is good, what is evil, what is right and what is wrong,
This seeker is me—
Why won't you come along?

1
COLLECT ARROWS

WHEN THE WORLD IS DARK, I find my greatest source of light. It's days before the trip. Without an alarm, I look at my watch on the bedside table. It's 5 a.m., my favorite time to write. My mind is lucid when the moon still shines; all is quiet, and I listen to the birds begin their gentle chatter. I open my computer and check my final grade for my master's curriculum writer's workshop class. Tears well up in my eyes as I lean closer to the screen. I read my professor's message again:

> *If you can write through this time, you can write well through anything. The time has come to write your own story, as you see it now.*

For the first time, I'm seriously validated by another writer. But this is more than validation. It's encouragement, which conceivably is more important. Validation means the work you've done is indeed as good as you believe. Encouragement can bring a soul in need from despair to hope, and it only takes a few simple words: *You are worthwhile.* Encouragement can change the entire trajectory of somebody's life. My professor's honest words may very well have changed mine. I paste the message to the top of a blank Word document as motivation surges through my being. His words won't go to waste. Thoughts stream through my fingers and onto the screen as if I'm in a flow state where time becomes nonexistent. *I begin to type.*

Writing helps me understand the world in a way I've never been able to otherwise. Life is too beautiful to let slip away; maybe I didn't know how to hold on to it before. In a year when the world has seemed bereft of meaning, writing has given me a way to make sense of what we're experiencing. As individuals, we've questioned whether to make our voices heard. There's pressure to speak up, even if we don't understand what's truly taking place. Is that better than staying quiet and safe in the shadows? With so much noise telling us what we should do and what we should think, it's difficult to know what we believe in ourselves.

Instead of turning to the news, I've turned to the page; instead of letting fear in, I strive to let my faith in humanity spill out from my pen. In the darkest days, I just want to inspire others through words of encouragement, online. But even more powerfully and perhaps more difficult, I want to inspire others in person. In the lightest days, I'm grateful for every breath I take. I've found my greatest sense of self by merging these two realities into one cohesive being. That's what I feel, and that's what I'm going to follow.

IN 2020, THE WORLD BEGAN its seismic shift towards a future in need of change. Everything seemed normal until it wasn't anymore. Our modern day stands upon the crumbling facade of an outdated paradigm, and it took a pandemic like Covid-19 to make us stop and ask: *Is this the best that we can do?* In December 2019, the World Health Organization's Country Office in the People's Republic of China picked up a media statement by the Wuhan Municipal Health Commission from their website on cases of 'viral pneumonia' in Wuhan, People's Republic of China.[1]

In the United States, Covid-19 (an interchangeable term along with "the coronavirus" and "the pandemic") became a reality in March 2020, when the first stay-at-home orders were observed. I wondered what role I would play. My older brother Duke and I moved back home with my mom in Malibu, California, to be together as a family.

"You have to tell them," my mom would say when she'd see me staring into the heavens, lost in thought with a furrowed brow. With our previous reality in shambles, I wondered what steps I'd take next. I questioned how I would break away from working with my best friend Morgan as a real estate agent in Los Angeles.

"You're making yourself sick." My mom is the voice of reason. The thought of letting somebody down has always eaten at me. But the thought of letting myself down by not following my dream became unbearable. If we're lucky enough to find something that makes us come alive, it will make us sick in our mind, body, and soul not to follow it.

That something exists for all of us, yet we settle; we do what's realistic, what society deems *"the smart thing to do."* We join the rat race like everybody else because that's what we're led to believe is a necessary step in our modern culture. I'd rather fail miserably with my heart on the line, giving my dream everything I have, than live in regret for never taking a leap of faith. If I were going to dedicate the entirety of my being to writing, during Covid-19 would be the time to do it.

Order makes us comfortable. Order is when things go exactly the way we imagine. Order comes from planning for the future so we know what's coming. Order comes from playing it safe. I've had order my entire life. Now it was time to step into chaos and the great unknown—the place we must venture into if we strive to realize our full potential. I was stepping away from working with my best friend every day and closing a chapter of growth I'll treasure for as long as I live. But I felt like I was being pulled in opposite directions. It was time to make a change. When I did, a weight lifted from my shoulders. I sat at the kitchen table of my mom's house overlooking the Pacific Ocean and let ideas flow from my fingers from dawn until dusk. I was no longer merely writing on the side, but as a full-time writer.

OVER THE SUMMER, the sound of ripping seams could be heard reverberating throughout the United States. Protests, violence, and unjust death made each sunny day feel dark and morose in the shadow of a dividing nation. Writing became a way to develop my perspective on the situation. I needed to see the good; I had to find it somewhere, and that somewhere came from within. Pandemics have changed the world for thousands of years, I recognized, while curiously looking back through history to garner an understanding of how we've made it through times like this before. This one is different, however. The world as a whole has collaborated to eradicate this virus. The pandemic has forced every one of us to take a step off of the hamster wheel to ask: *What truly matters to me? If I might die tomorrow, what will I fill the rest of my day doing?* As a society, we've spent more time with our families. That is a reason to cherish this pandemic and what it's given us. But it has by no means been a straightforward transition.

We have confined our lives to within the walls of our homes. At times, this has felt intolerable. But maybe this period has occurred as an opportunity to look within ourselves. Suddenly, while folding a shirt, doing the dishes, or opening a book that has sat on the shelf for years collecting dust, a reflection comes to mind. In the early days of the pandemic I was focused on my writing projects, Duke was at work on his acting endeavors, and my mom was doing her best to keep the ship afloat. One night, I delved into conversation with my mom and brother as we sat around the wooden table that had become my writing domain. In early summer, the sun radiated golden light late into the evening. The sky was yellow and deep blue; the water glistened and reflected the few idle clouds.

"I wrote a story about us surfing, Duke," I said over the sounds of the TV in the background and the clinking forks and knives. "It's called *Finding Solace Riding Waves.*" I started to read the story I'd been working on that encapsulated what I was feeling. I read through each line with a shaky voice:

"I'm going to miss you, man, a lot," I said, holding back a flurry of emotion. "I'm going to miss this. I wish we'd surfed together more often." My throat quaked while I read; I took a long pause. I could feel my mom was on the verge of tears as well. At the heart of the story, I find the strength to tell my brother that I want to move to Japan to begin my career as a travel writer. But I couldn't go on. I broke down and cried over my plate of chicken and brussel sprouts.

"It's all good, man!" Duke said in his jovial way that makes me feel like we're kids. But we're not. His ability to keep his joy throughout this often daunting journey of life fills me with sincere gratitude; I am blessed to have him as a pillar to lean upon. I needed to hear his words.

"I know this is what you want to do, so do it." I pulled myself together and smiled as I wiped my eyes with my dinner napkin. It hadn't been the three of us together in a long time—my mom, brother, and me. I suppose it all became too much: the longing to follow my dream yet not knowing exactly how; the anxiety about what the future might hold; the feeling of being back in high school. We, or perhaps *I* stopped trying to be strong. I let go. This year has been a pause in time full of many moments like this one, separate from reality, yet perhaps more real than anything we called *living* before.

IN THOSE EARLY DAYS, TIME—the minutes and seconds which usually fall through our hands like water—had unraveled. Life at that very moment, and every moment since, has been about family. Perhaps we were asking questions of the universe independent of one another, but we were learning about who we are together as one. That's the wonder of it all. There is no point when life becomes effortless and we can finally take a breath of fresh air. We must simply learn how to breathe as we endure. In twenty years, I'll look at pictures of this memorable season and wonder, *Where has the time gone?* Who are we really, but the collective moments of yesterday? We are not only our physical body: our laugh, our smile, the look of our eye, or the way we walk. We are our thoughts, our emotions, our dreams; we are our past that only we have the power to recollect. One day this year will be nothing but the past, but should we let it be?

Every time we see our friends it has felt like a special event *because it is.* The strangest thing of all is only seeing people's eyes. Covering three-fourths of our faces with a mask has become the norm. When we pass one another, it feels nearly impossible to connect, no matter how badly I want to tear the cloth from my face and reveal that there is indeed a person underneath.

During this time, I've found tremendous solace by immersing myself in nature by whatever means possible. I've realized that the answers to the perennial questions of our existence are out there. They're in the rustle of the trees and the wisps of the clouds, the patterns of a stone, and the rushing, meditative sounds of the rivers. In falling into nature's embrace, we reflect on what we foster within our own souls. We contain the world within us. We're able to withstand the winds of tumultuous change. We are microcosms of nature, the planet, the cosmos; we persevere through the tests of time.

I aim to garner inspiration from the natural world. I'm ready to feel what it is like out there during this time of tremendous change. There's a desire in me to get in touch with the spirit I foster within my bones, and I know no better place to do this than in the cold, mysterious depths of the natural world. *The time has come to tell your story, as you see it now.* This book is a story of me, striving to find my way when it feels like there's no clear path to tread. It's also a story of us. This isn't a time to forget—it's a time to remember, forever and always.

Our experiences are arrows on our backs to draw upon in the heat of life's battle. They will always be with us. Whether regretful, beautiful, solemn or courageous, our memories are there to fortify us for the rest of our lives. To collect arrows is to live in gratitude for every step of the journey. No matter what happens, we'll always have a quiver of experience and our spirit as a bow. Each day is a memory that we get to shape and craft. We're sharpening the arrows to stow on our backs with every second we appreciate life for the gift that it is. This year is a collective arrow for humanity. At the end of 2020, I'm ready to embark on a solitary road trip through California and the Pacific Northwest, to dive into my past, better understand the present, and prepare for a brighter future.

These are my arrows of youth. Now let me take a step back.

Arrows of Youth

The Way of the Warrior Poet

I heard about this Warrior Poet;
He moves through life with grace.
He acts on his intuition,
Peace commands his face.
It may appear he doesn't feel:
No outward love of life,
Transcendent highs or wicked lows,
No single trace of strife.
Beneath that stoic countenance,
A world one cannot see,
This type of force, a gale wind,
Contained in energy.
It is the sky, it is the Earth,
It is the early morning moon,
It is the mountains, drops of rain,
A subtle hearty tune.
And all that's dead and all that breathes,
And all that lives to fight,
This is the Warrior Poet's way,
To be a guiding light.
Through actions,
He does seldom speak,
If only through a smile,
Connected to the past, it seems,

Within is but a child.
One who is strong and
One who cares,
He loves with all his heart,
If he had just one last day,
To leave his lasting art—
He'd want to spend his time with you
To make you feel alive,
To see the world as magical,
Before he'd say goodbye.
And through the struggle
And the pain,
The Warrior gives every last drop,
Of what he has and who he is,
No way to make him stop.
I heard about this Warrior Poet,
Asked where it is I'll find him . . .

Look to the stars, came a small voice,
To understand the choice;
It may be dark, but you will see,
He's every drop of you and me.

2
THE BEAUTIFUL VOID OF DARKNESS

F I WERE THE LAST PERSON ON EARTH, what would I do? I like to think I'd marvel at the dark depths of the evening sky. I'd watch the sun fade into nothingness, and then maybe I'd stay there, just sitting, with nowhere else to go. If nothing else mattered, if there was nobody else, I'd focus on my breath. I'd feel it enter my body and move through my limbs, filling every fiber of my being with the spirit of the wind. I'd walk—not fast, but slow—and then I'd stop to look around. Or I might walk for miles and miles, exploring the treasures of the Earth. I'd laugh as loud as I possibly could or scream from the top of my lungs. I'd cry, I'm sure of that, tears of pain and tears of joy, ecstatic joy.

I like to think I'd do something meaningful every day that brought beauty to the world—beauty like a ladder into the sky, something that transcends our reality. Maybe I'd arrange some fallen leaves to put a smile on my face. Then I'd watch them blow away. Would I work so hard or care so much? Would I worry at all about things I can't control? Or would I stare into the stars and imagine other galaxies—planets, rocks, wandering celestial souls, like me? I'd lose myself connecting the infinitesimal dots in space, those unimaginable distances apart that, when transfixed upon like dust in an eye, send me deeper into my own depths. I'd swim far out to sea just for the challenge, and I'd float there, no longer on land where I'm comfortable, but in never-ending translucent blue.

I'd miss people so very much. I'd miss my family and friends more than anything, but even just a stranger. I'd miss anyone I've ever called an enemy. And then one day, when I'm lost in thought, perhaps I'd run into another traveler who thought they, too, were the last person on Earth. Then I'd find myself again as I looked into their eyes. I wouldn't care who they were or how they'd arrived here or where they'd come from; I'd just want to know them. We'd look into the sky together and wonder what we're really doing here, floating, listless, in this beautiful void of darkness.

I'M NOT ALONE, but the question makes me consider what matters in life. Sometimes we must separate ourselves from the noise and step into solitude to understand who we are. We're more than just our body. We're more than just our thoughts. The body allows us to move through the world; we see another human being and the first thing we recognize is the body. Is it open or reticent? Is it relaxed or uptight? The body is physical, intelligent, and able to be worked on like a marble statue through diligence and will. We identify with our body because it rep-

28

resents to others who we are and where we've been. It holds physical signs of our past, scars from traumatic experiences and falls from lofty trees; it shows age through silver hairs or lines on our skin like the cracks of parched wilderness. Our body is the vessel in which we move through life, but there's more to our existence than merely the physical.

LATE NOVEMBER, 2020. The beach is dark. I look up into the cool night sky. I'm at home in San Diego, California. It's a night as beautiful as any I've experienced in a long time. I stand on the dusky beach and watch the pink clouds float across the face of the crescent moon. The receding water leaves a reflective mirror on the sand into which I look and see a distorted version of me, a semblance of myself—*my essence*—washed away with the flowing tide.

Why am I still wearing headphones? I ask myself. Or is it me that asks? There goes the mind again, doing what it does. I take them out to listen to the sound of the crashing waves. I take several deep inhalations and close my eyes to go deeper within myself. Our breath is the first thing we're given when we enter this world. It will be the last thing to go when we leave. To feel the air enter and move through our body is to be physically alive; to learn to control our breath is to be conscious of the magic that exists within us. That magic is our spirit.

It emanates from every falling leaf and each crashing wave. It's stored in the rivers and the gentle streams and bursts from the light of dawn cresting the horizon. The magic of the natural world exists within each of us if we give ourselves the time and space to tap into it. I've never felt such a call to do so. With each passing day, I realize that what matters to me isn't what we call traditional success. At least not yet.

Someday, that could change. Success may bring happiness, but it may not. I need to know I'm living my life for the right reasons. I'm in search of meaning.

EARLY NOVEMBER. AUSTIN, TEXAS. Duke and I saunter through the Austin airport an hour before our flight back to Los Angeles. We're disheveled after a few days of debauchery with Duke's college buddies, but we have one more mission in the Texas capital. It's an important one.

"Excuse me," I raise my voice to get the attention of the lone clerk operating the convenience store. She turns and smiles at the two lads before her. "Do you have two copies of *Greenlights*[2] by Matthew McConaughey?" McConaughey is undoubtedly an iconic symbol of Austin. Given his vocation as an actor and writer, and seeing as Duke is an actor and I'm a writer, it's only right to pick up two copies of the book on our day of departure.

"Yes, *Greenlights*, do you have two copies? Mmhm. Oh, you do. Perfect." She hangs up the phone and turns to face us again. "Yes hun, down by gate twenty-four, they have two left." *Target acquired.* My brother and I sit in two swiveling chairs off to the side of the gate in front of the wall-to-wall glass window.

I pull out the book and assess the satisfying weight and matte finish, something I've done since I was a kid at a book fair. I don't recall precise moments when I read the books I loved as a kid. All I remember is the *feeling* of reading them—total enrapture. Time turned to dust when I was spellbound by my favorite novels. I remember the joy of going to a book fair and perusing the aisles, looking at the spines of the books and admiring their different colors. I would pull a book out of the shelf as I do now and assess how it feels in my hands. I'll open the pages and rub the paper between my fingers, noting the quality. A well-made book is a form of art. It isn't only what the words contain, but how they look on the page, how they weave together, how the cover evokes emotion, and how the colors add vibrancy.

I love every aspect of what makes a book beautiful. With every new book, I slip off the cover to see the color of the binding. It's a little thing that's just for me to know, like a secret that lays buried underneath the pristine facade. It's a simple joy; yet our simple pleasures make life worthwhile. The colors of the pages in *Greenlights* are green, black, and white. Besides the body of the text, some pages include handwritten notes, and others comprise meaningful poems. The book is a beautiful expression of genuine creativity. I begin to read.

I sporadically peer up from the page to watch the planes arrive and go. The weather outside is overcast and sultry. Flying seems normal, because it is. It's an everyday occurrence, from the sailing birds to the drifting clouds. I hope to never lose my wonder for the phenomenon of flight, something we take for granted now, yet which seemed inconceivable until the twentieth-century. When I look into the sky and see the red light flashing on the wing of a plane, a repeating sign that it's real, like the beating of the heart, I stop and appreciate what's taking place. This planet never sleeps. Planes land. Then they go. We're always up somewhere, moving, existing, living. There's nothing to fear.

THE GROUND THAT WAS HOME a mere minute ago turns into what the sky was prior. It is something to look and marvel at, but instead of passing planes, I watch the stoplights of microscopic cars inching along like an army of red ants. We're travelers, doing what we've always done. Previously in ships and trains, now in cars and planes; humans move ceaselessly across time as we rise nearer to the doorway of the vastness of space. For now, we stay within our realm.

Something about being in this abnormal state of flight, looking out of the window at the stillness of the world, fuels my imagination. I wonder what those around me think. We're quick to judge: how people look, how they act and treat each other, their mannerisms, and what they wear. But I've found this human experience to be much more enjoyable when we give others the benefit of the doubt. I smile and make a silly face at the crying baby beside which I always seem to be seated, hoping to cheer him up. I turn my headphones up a little louder. The flight attendant is a kind human being. He eases the uncomfortable passengers' worry with a joke, a smile, and an air of assurance. People like him make the world turn instead of burn. I touch down in LA and devour the book in three days.

Greenlights is an ode to life, a guide full of trials and signs that told McConaughey, *yes*, continue on your path. Catching *greenlights* means go. For him, solitary trips turned into *greenlights*. I close the cover of the book and a spark ignites. I know immediately that I have to plan an adventure. The Pacific Northwest strikes me like lightning and sets my soul on fire—I get goosebumps as I study a map of the United States. I derive inherent joy from looking at a map and planning my route, knowing that soon, I will not be looking at a screen, but hopefully, a tangible piece of paper that'll sit on the dash as a talisman of travel.

The more I explore the country's varied landscape and cities, America becomes increasingly alluring to me. The cities, towns, and cultures of the country each have an identity, something my great-grandfather Max Lerner treasured, specifically his native New York. Sanford Lakoff writes in *Max Lerner, Pilgrim in the Promised Land*:[3]

> *In one lyrical piece written in 1943 when the wartime ban on lighting was lifted for New York, he [Max] celebrated his love of the city's distinctive neighborhoods as a "mosaic of memories and images." "I think it is a heart, and I mean this in a literal and not a sentimental sense. In almost every culture, the town or city is built around some center to and through which the blood of the community flows. It may be the agora, the commons, the pub, the crossroads store, the market square, the green or the church. But in each case it is the pole between which and his home a man can move. It is a place of quiet talk, of bantering association."*

Max was a writer, a teacher, and a political commentator active during the twentieth century. I feel connected to Max through the passions we share for a lifelong pursuit of knowledge and respect for the written word. Max was an inquisitive human being who fostered an unwavering zest for life. He wrote countless essays on politics in the twentieth century, as well as the book *America as a Civilization: Life and Thought in the United States Today*.[4] This book was the leading authority on American politics after Alexis de Tocqueville's 1830s exploration of society in the nascent nation: *Democracy in America*.[5] His curiosity drove him to do extraordinary things, and it's the same curiosity that drives me. To remain inquisitive, open, and passionate to learn about the people and places that characterize the world makes life a never-ending quest of discovery.

All the cities of the world have their heart and distinguishable essence. I long to see each one. However, the world is on lockdown. I'll wait to do it right. I start to plan. *It has to be a road trip; the time of year is perfect, early winter.* I read that Washington's Olympic National Park is one of, if not *the* most beautiful national park in the country. This is saying something, considering the grand diversity of the United States' landscape and the sixty-three national parks that enrich the country. A trip to the very top of the Pacific Coast will inspire me in a myriad of ways.

I fervently believe travel changes us. A 2018 study by a team of social scientists at Rice University, Columbia University, and the University of North Carolina found that living abroad can clarify your sense of self.[6] Traveling puts us in uncomfortable situations where we're required to ask: *Who am I, and how will I react in this environment? Will I seek the help of a stranger by speaking up? Will I act courageously if need be?* We're exposed to new people, fresh ideas, and foreign landscapes that excite our senses and make us come alive.

MAX LERNER

TO GROW OLDER means accepting that I do not know, really anything at all. That's why I must go. There's a beauty in the unknown, as it signifies something, perhaps unattainable, to always continue striving towards. To admit we do not know is to awake in the darkness. In the darkness, we are open to learning. We use our hands and feet to navigate the uncharted terrain; our senses go on high alert and we change. To believe we know precisely what the world is like is to never open our eyes at all. It is dark in this space too, but there's nowhere to move. I long to explore the world in a way that helps me better understand my place in it. I'll never fully understand, but traversing into the unknown makes life a daring adventure.

We're given roles when we're young: son, daughter, student, artist, athlete, employee. We identify with these roles because there's hardly any other choice. We assume the roles are who we really are and build a structure based on this illusory foundation. But one day we wake up, and, if we're fortunate, we realize that there's more to life than these fixed roles.

I long to take a step closer to my ideal life by adhering to the passion placed in my heart. It may be scary in the darkness, but it's okay to be afraid. It's quiet, it's still, yet it pulses with the energy of existence. The only way to illuminate the darkness is to drop preconceived notions and let our light guide the way. The further we go within ourselves, the more we're exposed to alternative possibilities, opportunities, and ideas. What was dark before can now, just maybe, be seen.

Once we're there we can't go back, for there's nowhere to return. The darkness doesn't matter anymore. That's when we must take the next step, and the next, and the next. In the darkness we find who we truly are. All I know is that I do not know. I do feel something, however, and I'm going to follow that feeling.

I DECIDE TO BEGIN in Yosemite National Park, a jewel of California that will assuredly be crisp and nourishing in the early winter. From there I'll travel to the Redwoods National Park, an assemblage of coastal forests home to trees as old as Christianity. My trip will extend north into Oregon, where I'll stop in Portland to visit a good friend who calls the pioneer city home. After Portland, I'll cross into Olympic National Park to explore its sundry natural wonders, from rain forests and icy lakes, to rugged beaches and snow-topped mountain passes.

My route home will take me to Neskowin, a small and rugged town on the Oregon Coast; Fort Bragg, where I'll visit Thatcher, my college roommate and one of my best friends; and then I'll finish in San Francisco, a city that holds a special place in my heart. Everything I am and everything I strive to become tells me that this trip is more than a good idea; it's something I have to do. I need to be alone with my thoughts amongst the trees and the cold winter air; I need to reflect on what I genuinely want to do with my life at this pivotal moment in human history. With an unfaltering grin, I tell my dad and my stepmom, Eileen, the news.

"I'm going to drive from San Diego up to Olympic National Park, stopping at Yosemite, the Redwoods, and a few spots in Oregon on the way up and down." I smile as big as I can at the dinner table while attempting to explain to my dad and Eileen this spontaneous idea that's possessed me. Subtle changes take place on their faces as the words passionately pour from my lips. *What's going through my dad's mind?* I wonder.

Worry, at first, but then perhaps it's pride. He was once in my shoes: a kid who sought to find a purpose beyond the trivialities of everyday life. My dad heeded the call, and that's what made him who he is. His openness to new experiences has never wavered. He's the greatest inspiration a young man seeking adventure could have. Eileen gives a comforting smile; she's always been a creative spark in my life. Almost better than anyone, she knows I aspire to capture the essence of what it means to be alive.

"That sounds amazing; I'm so happy for you." I can tell she knows that this is more meaningful to me than anything I've done before. Often, meaning comes from what's right in front of us. Seldom do we take the time to stop and grasp it.

"Won't it be snowing up there? Are you going to get tire chains?" asks my dad. I smile at his practicality. Obviously, it's needed.

"Don't worry, Pop, I'll get them."

"Does your car need an oil change?"

"Not sure—*maybe?*"

"Will restaurants be open?"

"Not sure, but I'll bring my own food."

"Well, if it sounds good to you, it sounds good to me." He always comes around. "Just be safe, champ."

Arrows of Youth

Regularly Tested

Patience,

Waiting,

At once I thought I knew.

For what appeared so badly wanted

Now no longer true.

A virtue

Regularly tested,

A flame that burns naught slow,

Though what seems so important now

Is better to let go . . .

3
IT ALL HAPPENS FOR A REASON

CAL POLY, SAN LUIS OBISPO. 2013.

"I don't know what to do Mom, I hate journalism." I laid on my bed, staring up at the ceiling of the room I shared with Morgan. "It just doesn't feel like me. I wish I just had a test to study for where I knew what I had to do, and if I did it, I'd get a grade; if I didn't do it, I wouldn't."

"I know it's not easy, just be thankful for everything you're learning." I knew she was right. At the moment, however, I felt like I didn't belong. *What was I doing in journalism?* I never even wrote a journalism paper in high school, yet I decided to study journalism for four years.

"I hate calling police chiefs and city council members to interview them. It just seems like I'm a nuisance; you know I hate bothering people."

"You'll look back one day and be glad you stuck with it, trust me."

FALL. 2020. I stuck with journalism (partially because Cal Poly made it nearly impossible to change majors, but that's another story) and left with a bachelor's degree and a disheartening relationship with news-reporting. During my time as an undergrad, I interviewed a wide range of subjects: a local police chief and city council members, dairy farmers (it is Cal Poly), student entrepreneurs, and a top media executive, among many others. Like my mom predicted (moms are usually right), my fateful days in journalism were for a reason. First, I learned how to write, even though it felt grueling. Second, I grew determined to get out of my comfort zone and embrace my fears.

If one believes in destiny, then the letdowns, the blissful moments, the people we meet, and the leaps of faith are all preordained. It's as if these crucial experiences are out there in the universe, waiting for the correct combination of timing and boldness to ignite like the Big Bang. It's up to us to provide that flash of life. Perhaps when it's all said and done, we'll be standing atop some victorious mountain peak where we're able to stop, turn around, and take a long breath of cold, glorious air. I want to look down as my heart beats out of my chest and say: this is what I've conquered.

Those were the points when I thought I couldn't take another step, yet I dug my heels into the mud and pushed forward through the night. I'm looking up at the dense clouds that shroud my future in mystery from my current perspective. What lays beyond those icy pillows in the sky is far from clear—but I will climb, if only to provide that spark. I believe there's meaning to the uncertainty. At any moment, we're capable of changing our lives with a daring leap of faith. When we get comfortable being uncomfortable, genuine change occurs. When we imagine that every human connection is for a reason, we'll live with greater love and passion in our hearts, for every conversation could propel us on a new venture.

This life can be a constant uphill battle if we take it on ourselves, but it doesn't have to be a solo ascent. Some people want to help, and those people are vital. These are our friends, our family, the people we love. Yet some people will challenge us—these are the relationships we struggle with, for we don't always see what benefit they provide. Yet, the people who challenge us can be the very people we need.

One of these people was my college journalism professor, a man who looked exactly like Sam the Snowman from the original *Rudolph the Red-Nosed Reindeer* Christmas special. However, he was quite the opposite of a comforting Christmas special—at least in the beginning. I'll call him Sam. Sam taught several entry-level journalism courses and specialized in upperclassmen courses. His trademark course was media law, a class that all journalism students had to take after deciding they'd put it off for as long as possible.

When I took the class, I remember how the students would shuffle in, awaiting his first few words. Suppose you didn't read? *Game over.* If you didn't speak during a discussion, he'd call on you. Many failed his classes multiple times before finally passing. Some left journalism altogether after having him as their freshman news-reporting professor. As a young reporter, Sam covered the law in 1950s Texas—that was *his* freshman news-reporting class. He garnered a perspective of life I can't imagine.

But underneath that tough, hard-hitting newsman exterior, there was a kind man, one who sincerely cared about the next generation of journalists. As he said, he believed in truth and democracy. That he looked exactly like Sam the Snowman helped take the edge off, too. Sam always insisted on getting more information for our stories, perhaps by taking a trip to the municipal courthouse to speak with the District Attorney, my favorite weekend activity. Or he'd insist we call sources directly.

That was the reasonable course of action, but I felt like I was wasting their time. Why would anyone want to talk to a naïve college news reporter? Each unwanted call and each rejected story idea strengthened my determination. Those timid days were turning me into a writer. After class, Sam would go over each student's story one by one. He'd bring out a large roll of paper from the art department and carefully unroll it on his desk like an Egyptian papyrus scroll. With a yellow pencil, he'd draw a giant inverted pyramid, to represent the structure journalism stories follow: *the most newsworthy details on top, and the general info on the bottom.*

We'd go over every paragraph at his wooden standing desk, where he'd scratch through the unnecessary words as if he were crossing names off a mob hit-list. Through this one-on-one time, I'd nervously tell him a little more about myself. I didn't see myself as a journalist. But a few years later, through several seasons of swimming just to stay afloat, everything I've gone through has led to where I am on my journey. In the years I interacted with Sam, he impacted my life in a way that maybe he'll never know. I strongly considered changing majors, but I didn't. I continued to provide the needed spark just by showing up. I believe that is fate.

Without those challenging years, I wouldn't be where I am. I want to travel the world, tell stories, and live my life as I see fit. I dream of connecting with others through writing and reading and pursuing the passions placed in our hearts. Perhaps that will change in five years. But right now, all I can do is continue looking up and taking this climb day by day. Wherever you are, Sam—probably retired and kicking back—I hope you know I now thrive on what I feared in those college days.

Sam, you taught me how to use the written word as a guiding light to illuminate the darkness in ourselves and the world. Sam wasn't so scary after all. Nobody is. Perhaps we are destined to meet the people we meet, the ones who we fear, and the ones who need us more than we think we need them. Each connection is an opportunity to take another step uphill through the fog and the sweet-smelling trees. All we can do in times of uncertainty is to keep taking steps by doing our best in every circumstance. It may take a leap of faith or a whim of trust, but I say: *Why not believe it all happens for a reason?*

When I graduated, I bounced around from job to job, experimenting to find a path that I actually connected with on a deeper level. But nothing spoke to me. Fashion and style have always been a big part of my life, so I tried working in a clothing store. While there are skills to be attained from working in jobs like retail, I couldn't stand using my time during the day to progress toward a paycheck—I wanted to be working toward something meaningful to me. There's absolutely nothing wrong with working retail and getting a paycheck, but I felt a hole in my spirit that money and security couldn't fill.

I wrote on the side to decipher what I was feeling. I created a blog on Medium.com and found that writing about traveling was my favorite thing to do. On every trip, I'd write a story about my experience. Over time, I found it was something I deeply enjoyed. One of my innate callings is attempting to capture a place's history and culture through pictures and words. I strive to illustrate what it's like to be there, wandering the streets, led by our five senses. I hope to impart to my reader a moment in time in a piece of the world hitherto unknown to them. Then maybe they'd want to go there with a mind open to change, too.

When the coronavirus struck, I began taking incremental steps to attain the life I envisioned for myself. The year 2020 was the most creative year of my life, and while the coronavirus has swept the rug from under us as a planet, I feel that it's sent me on the path of learning, exploration, and discovery that I'm born to traverse. I created The Dare to Dream Podcast with Gregory, one of my best friends who also left his job at the beginning of quarantine. We both believe that there isn't any time to waste living a life that's not our own. While we figure out what that means to us, we strive to inspire others to do the same. Yet, some of us never find what we're destined to do, and I believe it's because we don't give ourselves the time and room to ask questions. We're focused on success; we're compelled to keep up, but we don't know what success means to us. Before social media made the world one interconnected social ladder, one might only compare themselves to similar age groups in their hometown.

Now we're constantly fighting an uphill battle by comparing ourselves not only to our friends and those in our immediate sphere, but to the entire planet and those at the very top of their respective fields. Society's expectations to succeed weigh heavy on our shoulders. We're subconsciously led to think that it isn't enough to be a living, breathing, beautiful being of light with gifts, able to move at our own pace. We feel we must always do more to get ahead. To achieve this lofty goal of becoming the next millionaire in their twenties, we sacrifice happiness by throwing ourselves into careers we don't even enjoy.

We must open our eyes and wake up from somebody else's dream. We must find what makes *us* come alive. The more questions I ask of the universe, the more I understand that *the answers are in the stars*. It takes looking into the black emptiness of night to realize what we need to add or subtract from our lives. How can we get to know ourselves when we're running through the day from task to task, then, spending our downtime mindlessly scrolling to see what other people are doing?

Nature is the most surefire way to simplify our lives. I step out into the unknown and ask: *What am I compared to this?* When I ask this question amongst the majesty of the natural world, what's unimportant loses significance. What matters seems to rise to the surface. The natural world has always existed; every second, every minute, and every year, it changes—ever-so-slightly, but it does change. What matters to me is feeling a connection to the Earth that we call home. My human concerns dwindle as my spirit grows to match the natural world. I've never felt such profound energy in my heart, spirit, and soul. These are the incorporeal parts of our being that make us who we are.

He Knew He Could Fly

Nervous he lived, and nervous he wrote,
But he packed up his things, and he put on his coat.
Stepping out in the cold, his breath fresh in the sky,
He knew this was it—he knew he could fly.

He's leaving what's comfortable, what he knows as home,
What urges him on is a life of his own.
Each step that was taken away from that place,
Each step became harder, yet he moved on with grace.

Just a pack on his back, and a note in his pocket,
Clasped by a hand that he couldn't take off it.
The note it was written a time not long ago,
From a loved one who lives in what's always his home.

The note it was tattered, but its message was true,
The message read this:
We are always with you.

4
LEAVING HOME

ITH THE MOONLIGHT AS MY GUIDE, I tiptoe through the still, silent house to see if my mom is awake. Today I'm heading north. I crack the door open and peer my head halfway into the room, yet I can't see much in the darkness.

"Mom?" I whisper. Her soft voice comes from the bed; I can tell she's been waiting to say goodbye.

"Are you leaving?" The faint light from the living room enters through the open door.

"Yup, I'm about to take off," I reply, trying to withhold my exuberance.

"Okay." She pauses, as if something is pressing on her mind. "I just don't see why you have to go alone." Admittedly, these aren't the last words I expected to hear from my mom. I take a breath; I don't know if she can see the expression change on my face, as the sun is far from rising. Maybe I'd feel different in the light of day, but in this moment of darkness, the statement hurts. A few seconds pass; I feel frozen in time. It's as if this moment symbolizes our relationship, yet it's one that changes with each step I take towards living my individual truth.

Our relationship is built upon love. I know, regardless of anything else, this will never change. She cares, more than anything. There will be times in all of our lives when the world questions our decisions. Letting go of what the world thinks is an essential aspect of growing up, but when our family questions what we're doing with our life, we question who we are. Our family doesn't have to agree with everything we do. My family doesn't know how my heart longs to make a difference. How can they honestly know? It's an indescribable feeling that burns in me. They don't know how my spirit seeks adventure. They don't know how my soul wants to experience all that life can give and how I long to give it back.

I have to get out there to see what I'm made of; I won't live my life in fear. I can try to explain to my mom why this has to be a solitary trip, but maybe I don't need to. She's my mom. All the worry, anxiety, and fear derive from love. The pain turns into gratitude. I close my eyes and smile.

"I just do, Mom," I reply, weighing my words. "Everything will be fine, please don't worry." My mom used to tell Duke and me to have siblings when we're parents, so our kids will always have each other. It's sound advice, as I did always have a friend. When I'd discovered that Duke ran away from home (which meant hiding out in the bushes down the street for about four hours), I'd burst into my mom's room in a panic.

"Duke ran away again!" I was often more worried than she was.

"He'll be all right," she'd stoically reply. "Let him be alone for a while." If she panicked and went out searching for him, my brother would have won. My mom wasn't giving in. He'd be back when he realized she wasn't out looking for him. Of course it affected her. But my mom stayed steadfast and didn't show her worry, at least not to me. That's parenting, isn't it? Do whatever it takes to keep the peace and somehow bring light and love into your child's life? Hopefully, you've done enough to keep them out of trouble, you've shown them you care, and that you believe in whatever it is they do if they truly believe in it, too. And then, through the observance of your actions in the world, your kids float downstream on their own without hitting too many rocks along the way.

Nobody has it all figured out, not even our parents. When I came to understand this, everything changed. I used to wonder what it would be like to have multiple kids. How could parents manage it if they liked one kid more than the other? Wouldn't one always receive more attention? How could you make sure each one fulfilled their potential and received all the love, care, and support they need to succeed? It doesn't work out that way.

The parent doesn't need to *make* their kids anything. They don't need to assess that all their kids are being loved, supported, and nurtured exactly the same way. All the parent has to do is to be there. As a parent someday, I simply hope to be myself. By being myself, I intend to love my entire family with the same amount of passion and encouragement. But the parent doesn't need to worry. The kid will find their way if properly guided along. They will try and fail; they will take great leaps of faith, and there will certainly be things they fear.

There's no shortage of things to fear; it's a kid's noble duty to face them on their own. It's the parent's job to be there for support, no matter the kid's endeavor. Parents must guide and prepare their kids for the world, but each kid is on their own. Parents can try to give their children the best circumstances possible, but kids see with their own eyes, hear with their own ears, and feel with their own hearts. The perception kids develop through trial and error, through falling and rising, and daring acts of courage steer them along the rest of their journey. Everybody is trying their best—parents just as much as the kids. I know my parents have always tried to give me all the love that they could possibly manage. That's all we can ever do.

"I love you, Mom, don't worry. This is going to be great." I step to the edge of her bed and hold her close, grinning from ear to ear.

AT 6:00 A.M., I STOP AT MY DAD'S house on my way out of town. I pull into the driveway and see him moving something, a fold-up chair from here to there, tinkering as fathers do. He's already hours into his day, shuffling about. We're two early birds.

"Son!" He seems almost as eager as me. "You're going to have such a good time." He hands me a cup of coffee that exudes the warm scent of vanilla; we sit down in the fold-up chairs. I don't know if it's the coffee, but he can't stop smiling, and nor can I.

"It's the best driving by yourself! Do you need paper towels on the road? Wipes? Forks and knives?"

"That's okay, Dad," I reply, thinking back on our summer RV road trip where the excess of silverware and kitchen supplies rattled so loudly as we drove it sounded like a being in the heart of a thunderstorm. "I think less is more for this trip; I'm not trying to recreate the RV situation."

We both laugh out loud as we recall the hellish 115-degree days in the Arizona desert from our summer excursion. It was just me, my dad, Duke, and my younger brother, Eileen and my dad's son, Jesse. Jesse's in high school and is more passionate about running than anything else. I can't blame him. There's something about pushing your body to its limit—no machine, no gym necessary—just a kid chasing an opportunity that beckons in the distance. I'm chasing that thing, too; maybe it's freedom, or maybe it's a novel moment never before felt or experienced—a new personal record on the track, and the realization that you could always be something more.

When the temperature dropped on a cool, golden evening in Flagstaff, Arizona, we pulled the RV up to the periphery of the local high school track. Jesse eagerly hopped the fence while my dad, Duke, and I joked and watched the kid take off beneath the broad desert sky. It was a moment I'll always remember when my dad said through his actions: *Follow your heart, kid, and I'll support you. I'll take you to the local high school wherever we are, just to watch you run.*

The garage has turned into my dad's man-cave since the quarantine. This may be why he is so happy. He has a TV on the wall, a row-machine, spin-bike, and weights. Lined up on the far wall of the garage are our old surfboards and pictures of each family member engaged in some sporting activity; I'm midway through tossing a frisbee,

Arrows of Youth

for context. The garage represents all the man has ever wanted. He's a simple, cheery soul.

"Right, I get it," he says, smirking. I polish off the last of my roast and get up out of the neon beach chair.

"All right, Pop, I'm going to get going."

"Are you sure you don't want the paper towels?" he asks as if for the first time. Maybe I *do* need them.

"Okay, hand them over."

Just knowing that I'll have a fresh roll in my car makes him happy.

"Drive safe! Don't tailgate! Drink coffee, and pull over if you're tired!" These are his departing words; they are the best I'll ever hear, the ones I'll listen to ringing in my ears for the rest of my life.

Arrows of Youth

Nature's Magic

———

I watch the seasons come and go
Sultry summer, peaceful fall,
Nature's magic to bestow.
A winter morning's sun stays low,
A fire raging, cozy shawl
I watch the seasons come and go.
In spring, the smell of roses blows
A pleasant passing note to all,
Nature's magic to bestow.
As days pass by, comes change in tow
In our own lives we forestall
I watch the seasons come and go.
Time's a river, ceaseless flow,
The trees have grown and now stand tall
Nature's magic to bestow.
Back again, late summer glow
The moon, it gives its closing call.
I watch the seasons come and go
Nature's magic to bestow.

5
THROUGH THE GENERATIONS

THE GOLDEN LIGHT OF DAWN PERMEATES through-
out the canyon that I've been driving over for exactly a decade,
since high school. I reflect on how this morning was like a case study to
represent the different perspectives of my mom and dad. My mom has
encouraged me to foster deep spirituality and a longing to find peace
within myself. She studied spiritual psychology and has shown my
brother and me how the thoughts we choose to believe create our reality.

Just because we think a particular thought doesn't make it real.
Thoughts come and go, yet we decide what to latch onto. They can either be positive or negative—it's up to us to choose. At first, I saw her
statement as demoralizing. *Does she think I can't handle myself? Doesn't
she realize how important this is to me?* The mind immediately provided
me with a negative interpretation of her innocuous statement. But with
a simple change of perspective, I could see with clarity that she was

coming from a place of love. Life has been an absolute journey with my mom. She's the strongest, most interesting woman I know. She's wise like an owl and can often tell what's wrong with me when I'm upset, even when I don't know myself. When life has tried to dim her light, she has bravely shone on. My mom derives much of her humor and wisdom from her dad, Richard Russell. Richard was a brilliant man.

The stories I hear and what I saw of him proved this. He was quirky like my grandmother Constance, too. Richard served in WWII as a bombardier on B-25 Mitchell bombers with the 12th Air Force, flying and dropping bombs over Italy. When he returned from the war, he began selling ties and became intensely interested in the stock market. Richard was a writer who spent his days connecting with readers through his Dow Theory Letters.

The Letters covered the stock markets, bonds, metals, and economics. But that's not why his readers came back year after year. He wrote about everyday life. There's only so much you can write about the stock market. His readers got to know him through the Letters. When he died, many spoke at his funeral to share stories of the man who made them money, but also who entertained and delighted them.

My brother and I didn't know him on a deep level, and that's not something I regret. We did the best with what we knew as kids. I'll never forget the last time I spoke with him.

"HELLO?" I PICKED UP MY MOM'S CALL. It was unusually early for her back in California, and around midnight for me in Florence, Italy.

RICHARD RUSSELL ON THE FAR RIGHT; ITALY, WWII

"Hey honey," came her wavering, yet resolute voice on the other side. "Do you want to talk to your grandpa? It may be the last time."

Blood rushed to my cheeks as the wine I'd drunk that evening exacerbated my emotions. I didn't know what to think, so I answered.

"Yeah, of course." A few empty moments passed before I heard a sound. "Hi, Richard?" My voice was shaky and dry in the brisk midnight air. I stood by myself on the narrow cobblestone street in Florence, where I studied abroad as a junior in college. My friends were upstairs drinking wine and preparing to leave for a night out. I held the phone close to my ear, unsure of what to say.

"It's Vinny. I just want to let you know I love you, and I'll always remember the times we came over to your house and you drew us cartoons." Through the second story open window, I heard my friends' laughter. I could hear the footsteps of people walking along the River Arno a block away. I could see my breath fade into the night sky. But I didn't hear my grandfather's voice.

"I'll miss you; I hope you know that." I hung up after another word with my mom. I didn't know how to re-enter the party. These were my final words to the grandfather I barely got to know. *I'm speaking to him now through the words on the page.* Richard Russell was a writer, as was his mother Hortense Lion. Writers connect through their words on the page that are often too difficult to articulate. But just because we leave the physical world doesn't mean we're gone. I have an entire life to make up for the time I didn't get to know him. The older I get, the more I want to get in touch with the family I hardly knew.

Richard collected an impressive number of cacti at his home in La Jolla, California. They were the first thing we noticed when we visited him as kids. One could find every shape and size in the brick courtyard of his home, baking in the Southern California sun. To me, they all looked the same. I never understood what he loved so much about the boring and threatening plant. Now I think I understand.

"They're fighters, like me," is what he always said in his high-toned, raspy voice. When we visited, he would draw us cartoons. These were sketches like ones in a 1950s *New Yorker* article—a profile of a face quickly etched on a scrap piece of paper lying around. He was an artist in more ways than one. He was a fighter, a lion, and a Russell. I'm honored to have the name Vincent Russell Van Patten, after him. To learn about my family, my grandparents, and the generations before them is to study history. My blood changed their respective eras for the better, one book, letter, and person at a time.

MY DAD HAS INSTILLED IN ME a fervent call to adventure. With him, I feel the need to seek the nature of what makes life a joyful ride. It's doing what others aren't: making life delightful, creating my own reality, and not waiting for permission to do what I know is right. I think of my dad and the perspective he's given me. It makes me who I am. My appreciation for the subtle charm of a park, the invigorating feeling of the frigid ocean, the timeless smell of a fresh red clay tennis court—no matter where we are, together or apart, this personal admiration for the world binds us.

When I travel, a hunger stirs within me to rise at the crack of dawn. I come alive when the stars remain shining over an unknown land where I'm free to explore and let my mind and spirit drift through the cool morning streets. I savor each breath of tranquility and embrace the rain

Arrows of Youth

falling from the fleeting darkness. A cloudless day is a gift. But I share with my dad the appreciation for gazing out a window, listening to the calming dullness of a steady rain.

As a son, I look to my father for guidance. I'm blessed to see my dad as successful, knowing that whatever trials I'm enduring, he has been through his own and has come out stronger. I consider him successful because he lives to share his blessings: *he's happy*. When we're young, our parents seem invincible. Nothing can penetrate their well-honed armor formed from years of navigating trials and victories. When I've had questions, I've gone to my parents like a troubled youth seeking the prophecy of an ancient oracle.

My parents will always be my parents, and I will always be their son. But I'm no longer just a kid. To them, I know I'll always be. But life continues each day in which the sun and moon rise and fall. With that comes a life of my own. Every day, I pick up my mighty brush and take a stroke at the blank canvas of life. When I sit down at the computer and put down my thoughts, take a walk and think about my purpose, or call a friend to be there for no reason at all, I take a swipe at the canvas. I don't know how the picture will look when it's all said and done. But it will be full of color; it will depict a life passionately lived.

My parents, too, have their own painting to do. In this season of life I've gone to them, hopeful that they could help elucidate the way through their experience of being young and full of questions. Indeed, they have always inspired me. However, it isn't necessarily through concrete answers. Sometimes being there, listening on the edge of the bed, is all we need to carry on. Through these moments, I've learned more about who they were, not only through a son's revering eyes, but as an honest friend, sharing in the experience of what it means to be human.

As a kid, I didn't want to see my parents as anything other than my parents. As an adult, they're infinitely more to me. They are human beings with just as much uncertainty, hope, and life to live. We're in this together, albeit in our respective seasons. Yet, no season is less demanding or less beautiful than another. The bare winter trees bereft of color and leaves are just as stirring as the burning red leaves of fall. Perhaps we're in different seasons. Yet, all seasons come, go, and coalesce with what comes next. We're all here on this Earth with a brush in our hand, filling a blank canvas with the colors of our spirit.

Our parents communicate to us the qualities that they believe will serve some greater good in our lives. They raise us and then we're set free to discover our mission, taking along what we've learned and preserved. Those lessons will always be there. Their love will always be there. More than what our parents deliberately instill in us, it's the observation of growing with them and subconsciously watching how they react to the world. We, as kids, make our own judgments of what's right or wrong. Eventually, I became mature enough to see that my parents learn from me just as much as I learn from them.

My dad made his way in the world through love and grit; I strive to do the same. There will always be things our family doesn't understand, but my dad understands my thirst for a solitary road trip. Family means love, regardless of if we understand or agree with each other. My mom worries about this trip because she wants me to be safe. My dad is excited for me because he knows I long to experience the world for myself.

Both feelings derive from love. There must always be love amongst family, for we share the same blood, history, DNA, and spirit.

I want to make them proud. But there will be times when we have to turn away from what our family, friends, and culture claim is the right thing to do. We have one shot at making our brief existence on this Earth something we'll look back on days before we die and say *I lived on my terms*. We have one chance to live our lives. This is my chance, and I'm taking it.

Arrows of Youth

When the Darkness Becomes Day

In our ever-changing world
Every spirit's individual,
The Earth's all-seeing eyes
Only know us by one name;
A shift in perspective to
Open up the mind,
One name—human,
One soul—I;
Enhancement of another's day,
Just by being kind.

Connected to the past is the
Man I want to be,
The reason we're here,
Open eyes that long to see.
Where I'm headed,
Don't know yet,
Although it's becoming clear,
That whatever land
I call my home,
I'm already here.

A destination I'm proud of,
Sunny day of inner peace,
Walking tall, standing strong
Atop this mountain of trials,
Each thrilling step
Takes me higher,
Miles, and miles.

Between us all a bridge of light
Spanning heart to heart,
Takes bravery to
Dance through life,
An essential art.

The first move is all that it takes,
Embrace the dark unknown,
'Cause when the darkness
Becomes day,
You'll see how much
You've grown.

6
THE LIGHT OF THE MOON

A SIX-HOUR DRIVE USED TO SEEM UNBEARABLE. But now, I appreciate the opportunity to do nothing but look out the window at the pale sky and passing desert. Seldom do we find ourselves alone without the need to do anything but think, listen to music or podcasts, or sit in our own silence. It's 9 a.m.; I look into the sky and notice the moon, still visible and unusually massive, as if it hangs by strings attached to the heavens.

How can we not believe in magic, a connection between our spirit and the universe, or even something more extraordinary when the moon lingers over our daily lives? It's unfathomable to consider the greater system we're a part of. This phenomenon, the going of the moon and the coming of the sun, mustn't become routine. It's part of the miracle of living, a simple moment to experience no matter where we are in the world.

In the late seventeenth century, Isaac Newton uncovered the laws of nature that act as an orchestrator directing the notes of our universe. People could hardly follow the mind of Isaac Newton, but he inspired them as he does me, someone who never took a physics class and by no means excelled in math. Through his laws of motion and gravity, the English physicist convinced the readers of his *Principia*[7] that we don't live in two worlds separated by some unfathomable barrier. We live in one coherent realm where everything has a purpose. Furthermore, the human mind can somehow comprehend this order that far precedes human existence and religion, dinosaurs and ancient beasts, and even our planet's creation. The English poet Alexander Pope famously wrote of Newton:

Nature and nature's laws lay hid in night. God said, "Let Newton be," and all was light.

Newton realized when an apple fell on his head that a specific force controls all that exists. Yet, he couldn't explain why or how. *"I do not know why, I do not know how, I only know that it is,"* said Newton.[8] With that comes perhaps his most impressive proposal—that he did not know. Newton admitted ignorance and proved he too was human, possibly the most perplexing creation of all. Worlds as complex as those above exist within each of us. But there's so much more to our existence; looking at the craters of the barren moon is a beautiful reminder of this.

We can look beyond the temporal and see something that's a part of our world but not, akin to the eternal human spirit. The natural world transcends one's era and creates a bridge between all of human history. I gaze at the same moon as Isaac Newton. It appears as a ball of light that sits in the sky like a pale stone. Without knowing why or what it's doing there, it seems to fade into our routine. You may drive to work on a regular Tuesday. *Look up! There's a rock floating in outer space right above your head!* The moon hasn't changed since Newton's day, nor have we. We're no different today than those who wandered and questioned, who struggled and loved with all their hearts, who only wanted to be free to think for themselves. But perhaps now we take the liberty of thought for granted. Newton's historic *Principia* played a significant role in ushering in the age of Enlightenment, which the eighteenth-century German philosopher Immanuel Kant defined as:

> *Man's emergence from his self-imposed nonage. Nonage is the inability to use one's own understanding without another's guidance. This nonage is self-imposed if its cause lies not in lack of understanding but in indecision and lack of courage to use one's own mind without another's guidance. Dare to know! (Sapere aude.) Have the courage to use your own understanding, is therefore the motto of the enlightenment.*[9]

Unlike the sun, we're able to look at the moon when it's enveloped in darkness; we're able to view something not of our world, a reason to believe that there's more to living than what we call routine—the act of going through the motions of somebody else's playbook. The sun shines down on us every day, but we can hardly see it. We know it's there, but like the inevitability of death, we'd rather not look at it straight on. The moon is different. Sometimes, I can't look away. It feels as though I'm up there looking down on Earth. From there, our problems seem so small.

THE MOON DISSIPATES as I draw closer to Yosemite. I take this moment as an augury that this trip will be full of connections between my spirit and the world we rarely think deeply about. It will be imbued with connections between myself, the universe, and other wandering souls. As I drive and watch the moon fade away with the rays of the rising sun, I listen to Vishen Lakhiani on *The Model Health Show with Shawn Stevenson*.[10] Vishen is the founder of the world's leading personal growth platform, *Mindvalley*, and one human being among many who have significantly impacted my life during the pandemic.

As I gaze into the expanse of the solar system, Vishen says something that's incredibly impactful. He discusses how we're part of an eight-billion-strong human colossus; like the cells of our body, each human being thrives off of the other. He mentions that according to Ed Diener of Harvard University, human connection—the most essential thing taken from us during this time besides our very life—directly correlates with an increase in happiness, while income is not highly correlated.[11] Vishen describes how he's working on creating an Earth flag because he believes nationalism makes us forget how connected we are. Our countries give us laws, identity, and a semblance of control, but what do they do to our overall psyche as human beings?

Divisiveness will destroy our planet if we continue on the path we're on. It's time to come together, not divide, yet much of the world still clings to a mentality that holds us back—*us* versus *them*, *nationalist pride* versus *global unity*. It's time for a paradigm shift where we make discussion, gratitude, health, education, and connection the main pillars to build our future upon, a structure of well-being for all that can support our ever-changing world no matter what adversity we face.

Instead of pointing fingers, how can we be more connected human beings who love who we are, are there for each other, and support and encourage one another through any difficult period? As human beings, we're asking the same questions we have since the beginning of humanity. We want to know where to find the answers to the mysteries of belonging, meaning, and pain. We've turned to drugs, numbing, and outmoded institutions to find the solutions. The amazing thing is, we can find the answers we seek in nature. We, as human beings, are nature. Nature is us. I am just as much the bark on the trees and the cold in the wind as I am every human being I come into contact with.

The sun maintains our energy; we eat from the soil. We are made of the bread eaten by our ancestors. Living in gratitude and fueling our bodies with the planet's natural, holistic medicine is the remedy for what ails us. This past year, as the traditional news institutions have sought to make money trying to divide us by imposing fear, the brave and joyful souls, including Shawn Stevenson, Vishen Lakhiani, and Aubrey Marcus, have encouraged us to come together to realize the power we contain within ourselves. It's time we see ourselves in one another, looking at the world through a different set of eyes.

Instead of blaming others because of our own insecurities, we must find compassion. There is nobody to blame. When we're able to foster empathy and kindness, the healing process begins. Aubrey Marcus put it beautifully when he had Shawn Stevenson on *The Aubrey Marcus Podcast*.[12] A man yelled at him for not wearing a mask outside of a grocery store. While many people would have retaliated from the verbal abuse, Aubrey did the opposite.

He felt compassion for this man. He asked himself *why* the man reacted this way. This man was likely fearful. It didn't stem from genuine hate, for he didn't even know Aubrey. But he felt threatened. Aubrey made it clear he isn't a wise sage who exudes love one hundred percent of the time. He's a human being, just like the man who yelled at him. We will all have moments of insecurity and doubt. But every human interaction is an opportunity to either move in the right direction or to take a step back. This pandemic is our rock bottom, although perhaps it has been painfully necessary to open up our eyes. There is no wishing the past was different in our own lives or the life of the planet. There's only creating a better future, one that starts with today. Humans aren't perfect—but we don't have to be. Instead of judging ourselves, others, and the world for not being like us, it's time we see we are all made of the same boundless energy. Let's figure out how to move forward together.

Through movement, there's nothing that can hold us back. Through our individual experiences, we derive meaning that can help move along the collective good. Often, we don't see the results of our efforts. The solutions, the recognition, the change—they don't come. That doesn't mean we should ever stop taking steps forward. In pursuing happiness and questioning who we are, there will often be no obvious answer other than an indescribable feeling in our heart and soul that tells us, *Keep going, take one more step.* So that's what we must do. With the light of the moon leading the way, the same moon that's always been, we'll never be alone.

Arrows of Youth

On That Day, I Met Somebody New

Initially I'm reticent
To tell all I withhold,
The inner workings of my mind
Not wanting to unfold.
It's taken time to build this wall
Containing who I am,
I work to keep its structure strong
In any way I can.
But then a stone or pebble falls and
Crumbles to the floor,
I met somebody new today,
You've opened up the door.
Behind your warmth of
Upturned lips,
So beautiful and dear,
Sleep lies and truths, a soul
Persisting, resolute and clear.
It's hard for me to simply share
The world I've come to know,
Within my heart I long to lead you,
Easier to show.
With words thought out and

Set in ink I hope that I can say,
The thoughts that filter
Through the wall,
I've built to keep at bay.
All that which makes me truly me is
Forced to stay inside,
My heart and soul which must now
Speak, no longer can I hide.
Break down this wall to
Reach the heart,
Which pounds beneath my bones,
It only takes a single question, a
Solitary stone.

I thought I didn't know you yet,
Your spirit new to me,
But once the fallen stones clear out
I'm now able to see—
That I have known you all along,
I know what makes you, you,
No longer walls obstruct the way,
I hope you see me too.

7

MARIPOSA GROVE

MY ASCENT INTO THE MOUNTAINS BEGINS AFTER passing through various old settler towns such as Coarsegold, Oakhurst, and Fish Camp. The ethereal nature of the morning has brought about a clear day. I pull into a gas station in one of these small towns—Oakhurst, I believe. A bell jingles as I open the door, and the woman behind the counter gives a casual glance.

"Hello," I remark as I walk past, hoping the woman can discern my smile from behind my mask. I try to smile enough so the shift in my facial structure will alter my eyes and perhaps the crinkle of my forehead so she'll see that there's a human under here. When wearing a mask, it takes a bit of extra work to make a connection—but it's possible. We must smile with our eyes with warmth and compassion. Smiling with our eyes tells the other person, *We're in the same boat, I'm not hiding—this is me.* How many interactions are there waiting to commence every day

Arrows of Youth

we leave the house? We often pass others like two ships on a foggy night, aware of the other, but not needing to connect. We might as well be phantoms. Like Ed Diener revealed in his study, we are social creatures who long for connection. Although it's proven that connection increases our happiness, it's easier to keep pretending like we only exist in our own limited world.

Connecting isn't always simple. We have to become vulnerable. We have to ignite a spark of change. Duke recently told me of an experience that speaks powerfully of his character. Duke is an aspiring actor and has been attending acting classes for years. He was in a class where another student seemed full of self-confidence, almost to a fault. Duke expected him to take the stage and crush his scene, but when we got up there, he froze. He couldn't remember a single line. Later that night, Duke saw the student by chance at a restaurant in our hometown of Malibu.

Duke knew this ostensible coincidence occurred for a reason. He had to say something to the man who seemed like a shell of his charismatic self before his debacle on stage. Duke gathered his courage and went up to tell him that there's nothing to be embarrassed about; all actors have times when they miss the mark, even the very best. Just laugh it off and move on. He thanked Duke and shrugged it off, not dropping his persona. They exchanged numbers and later that night, Duke got a text.

"God works in mysterious ways," the text said. He had decided he would quit acting after the embarrassing performance. He couldn't put himself back into that world after having an entire class *and teacher* laughing at him. *But Duke spoke up.* If he didn't, who knows what the other student would have done? Perhaps nothing; maybe something drastic. Duke very well may have saved his life with a simple gesture of compassion—an act of encouragement. When we speak up and say hello to another human, they may be taken aback. They didn't expect to talk to anybody today. Now, their entire plan has changed. They didn't see themselves straying from the well-trodden path of least resistance we call our daily routine. Most people aren't expecting a conversation.

A smile of recognition or a word of encouragement may very well save a human being from the dark depths of themselves. I stand in line to check out, holding a water bottle and a pack of winter mint gum. *What do I ask?*

"Has it been this nice all week?" *Easy enough.* The cashier glances up from the negligible task at hand and peers through the floating plastic barrier separating us. She reacts like I have asked her out to dinner. Reclaimed life flushes to her cheeks; she straightens her back. It's not complicated to ask a follow-up question. Yet, it means so much. Not only to others. Not only to us, either. It matters to the universe: the energy that binds us feeds off of our efforts to connect.

"Oh well, it's been pretty nice here the last couple of days, but it's going to be much colder if you're heading into Yosemite." She goes on for about a minute. I listen contently.

"Well, I hope I'm prepared!" I say with a grin.

"Have a great day, hun."

I ARRIVE AT THE YOSEMITE National Park entrance with little of a plan of how I'll spend the remaining half day. I pull up to the gate and am greeted by a sprightly young girl. She has a long, braided ponytail that falls down her back from under her Yosemite hat. It puts a smile on my face; I am happy to be here. I give as warm of a smile as I can.

"How's your day been so far?" I ask to break up the monotony of the process. She smiles back; I appreciate her authentic demeanor.

"It's been great! The park isn't as crowded as usual, which is nice." I like the sound of that. "Are you going to need a map?" She extends her hand, holding a map of the park with pictures of the different animals that call Yosemite home.

"Sure!" I exclaim, eager to prolong the conversation. I delicately unfold the map and scan from corner to corner until I realize cars are forming a line behind me.

"Well, thank you." There's a pressure when talking to girls. If the conversation is going well, the voice in my head gets louder—*Are you going to get her number? Where do you go from here? Don't let this slip away.* I'll feel a sense of regret or somehow that I've failed if I don't make that move. But what if there doesn't always need to be a next step? What if that connection of "Hello, how's your day going?" is all we ask?

Often I don't want to think about the next thing. I'm here; I'm present; I vibe with this girl's positive energy. Then it's over. I leave with a map; her, possibly a memory. She has a life, gifts, and dreams. I walk my own path with its daily decisions and regrets. All we share was a few moments where we had but an instant to make an impression. That's all that it had to be. Maybe our paths will cross again someday.

A week before the trip, I was in line at Trader Joe's picking up groceries. A six-pack of Anchor Steam Beer caught my attention in the checkout line—curse their jolly Christmas branding. Without reading the label, I threw it in my cart. Later that night I was at my desk writing under the light of a dim lamp. The room was warm and I felt the energy of the upcoming trip brewing within me. I cracked open an Anchor Steam and read the label on the bottle.

> *This is our Christmas Ale celebrating the Three Graces;*
> *three iconic towering sequoias from the Mariposa Grove*
> *in California's Yosemite National Park.*

I took a swig from the dark, nautical bottle and pondered the obvious application. The beer tasted as jolly as it looked, with hints of mulberry, chocolate, coffee, and spices.

> *This is only the second time in its 46-year history that multiple*
> *trees are shown together on the label, a fitting statement to*
> *symbolize togetherness and hope in a year when so much time*
> *has been spent apart. The Three Graces represent radiance, joy,*
> *and flowering—characteristics that we can all hold near during*
> *this unprecedented time.*

I thought to myself on that warm winter night: *It sounds like I'm going to Mariposa Grove to see the Three Graces.*

MARIPOSA GROVE: 0.5 MILES. Let's do it. I make my way around the roundabout and set off into Mariposa Grove. It's the early afternoon when the air is cool and the forest takes on a warm glow. I pull into the parking lot and quickly munch on a sandwich. Wait; there are zero reasons to rush. I lean back on the hood of my car and take in the sun beating against the black exterior. It feels necessary to stretch back as far as I can after hours of sitting. I listen to the birds chirping amid the surrounding sequoias and savor this moment to do nothing but think. I watch a family of about fifteen from across the lot. Several little kids are running around the dispersed coolers. The band has broken into separate groups and begins chatting amongst themselves. There's a time and place for everything. Right now, I want to be alone. One day I'll have a tribe like that to call my own. First, I have to figure myself out.

I leave for the trees, donning my puffy yellow jacket and my adventure pack, ready for an hour, maybe four, amongst the soaring sequoias. As I begin to stroll, I notice a soft light that slips through the branches in delicate waves. It feels like a fairytale in the afternoon sun. Speckles of light fall from the branches and work their way through holes in the leaves to create an environment of shade and light, rustling twigs, and ancient roots that surge from the Earth's soil. After about thirty minutes of switchbacks and trails, I come to some striking trees that have fallen and now exist as homes for various species.

Their exposed roots look like intricate alien enigmas woven like threads. I think of *The Overstory*[13] by Richard Powers as I stare into the eyes of these primordial wooden beasts. Powers entwines a handful of individual tales relating to the world of trees into one incredible story. The book made me see the trees as alive; they're communicating with each other. They aren't just towers of wood, but sentient forces. As I walk amongst the grove, I can't help but feel honored to be in their presence.

I continue meandering deeper into the forest until I come across Bachelor and Three Graces. The sequoias surround me like red pillars of earth soaring into the sky. I hang out below the Three Graces for a while, pondering the fact that a short while ago I was reading the beer label back in San Diego. Now I'm under their watching branches. *How did I get here, physically, mentally, and spiritually?* I stand under the Three Graces—I feel I'm meant to be here, but I don't know exactly why. It feels surreal, like anything I can think or imagine will come true. I feel like I have a superpower to realize my dreams.

Maybe I do. Maybe we all do. This trip was just a dream until I stepped into the unknown. What I'm doing is beyond what I can comprehend. I look up at the otherworldly trees. They look back down at me as if there's something I need to know, but the message won't come in words, just a feeling. There's a universal language found in nature, an energy that transcends species, borders, regions, countries, and cities. When something about the world awakens our soul, only this universal language can portray what we feel.

Poetry is this language, as all beings on this Earth speak as poets. The animals which dwell in mountain caves and linger atop flower petals; the plants which interact with the rising sun and lend beauty to the Earth; they speak through feelings, senses, songs of chirps and growls. Poetry is the best way I've connected with the subtle details of life and the mysterious character of nature that leaves me breathless. Sometimes the feelings that nature evokes are too complex to put into a logical sentence. Language is how we communicate what we feel, but language can't convey the depth, power, and majesty of life. Still, we can try.

Arrows of Youth

The poet doesn't need to explain through logic. To express what the poet feels, sometimes only one word is necessary, or a few words pieced together with intent like the three eloquent lines of haiku. Each word acts like stepping stones across a pond. Each step crosses the water, but it takes a hop, a jump, a leap of faith to get from one to the next. One looks at the pond and sees the stones emerge from the shimmering water; there's an unstructured structure, a connection between each stone, a bond between each word that takes traversing to discover. Each stone, each word, bears significance. The meaning underneath may not be apparent at first; still, the words matter.

When we think about poetry, what first comes to mind is a song-like rhythm; music without instruments to follow, only words, *sounds*, and their underlying meanings. Poetry evokes emotion in the reader or listener through how the poem sounds when spoken out loud, how it looks on paper, and the image that comes to mind when considering the words.

Poetic devices such as imagery, metaphor, repetition, rhyme, and tone can create an overall effect that can communicate a feeling more profoundly than well-constructed prose. Understanding a poem, however, often takes more than one reading. But immediate understanding is not the point of poetry. Sometimes we don't need to understand. We only need to listen. *I'm listening, trees; what is it you need to say?* No sound comes, but that doesn't mean they aren't speaking.

I HIKE UNTIL THE SUN FALLS LOW. I'm one of the last ones in the grove. This part of the day has a somber, elegant quality of its own. The sounds of the day fade and the heat lessens. The trees become ominous shadows looming overhead. I don't feel anxious as the day slips away. I feel at peace as the sunlight turns into night and the layers of natural sound amplify. I don't see many critters, but I feel they are here, watching me. The bugs and the leaves, too, go about their business as if I haven't entered their domain. They fall when they feel like doing so. They blow when it's time to blow. They take part in the season of change that our world undergoes—fall to winter, the old to the new, life, death, and rebirth.

It's dark as I drive through the valley to my Airbnb, which I'll be using as a home base in each location throughout the trip when not staying with friends. I could have camped, but with the inclement weather and quick turnaround time, from inception to commencement, this was the most feasible option. I don't know if the journey would have been possible without Airbnb, for it's an idea that has opened up a novel way for people like me to travel without needing to spend money on hotels. This one in Yosemite is like a communal hostel, and I know I'll warm up to it quickly.

I brought three books on the trip: *Eragon*[14] by Christopher Paolini; *The World Is My Home*[15] by James Michener; and *The Buddha and the Badass*[16] by Vishen Lakhiani. They are the ideal companions for a trip like this one. *Eragon* was one of my favorite fantasy books as a kid —it reminds me of the spirit that I once was, my essence, and my fire. I'm just a kid exploring his backyard, after all. *The World Is My Home* inspires me to work hard as a writer. James Michener enlisted in the Navy during WWII and traveled much of the South Pacific. He fell in love with the tropical islands and the caring, warmhearted people. His first book, *Tales of the South Pacific*,[17] sought to give a voice to the islanders and the servicemen he learned to love. He says:

> *For whom did I write as I sat night after night fighting the mosquitoes with those little bombs of insecticide the Navy gave us and pecking out my stories on the typewriter? Not the general public, whom I did not care to impress; not the custodians of literature, about whom I knew little; and certainly not posterity, a concept that simply never entered my mind. I wrote primarily for myself, to record the reality of World War II and for the young men and women who had lived it.*

I sometimes wonder where my love for literature and the world of words comes from. Sometimes it feels like it can't be me. I have to tell myself, *Yes, this is your life, so own it.* Only I know if I'm lying to myself. I recall the feeling of comfort that books brought me as a kid. That's what I feel now when I get lost in a story like *Eragon*. Wherever I am, there's nothing to fear. I open *Eragon* before falling asleep and read a passage that sparks tremendous joy in my heart. In the scene, the protagonist Eragon is learning to read. Think Middle Earth, where knowing how to read is a scarcity. Eragon pulls out an ancient text:

> *Eragon returned to his chair, holding the book gently. It's amazing that a man who is dead can talk to people through these pages. As long as this book survives his ideas live.*

As I read this, I envision the joy welling up in the author Christopher Paolini's heart and soul. Although the book is fiction, this is his thought. I am wonderfully baffled by this sentiment. We're both writers and share a love for books. Through books, we have access to knowledge from unimaginable eras in history. Books differ from any other medium, as they don't have to be anything other than the thoughts of another human being.

It takes willpower to get through a book—the journey may take a week, a month, a year. This weeds out those not committed to the slog. Writers write for those who are. What they get out of the book, what I get out of a book like *Eragon,* is a change in my day when I turn the page. I garner a shift in my perspective when I close the cover. A book becomes a part of me, for when I ultimately close the cover, the pages have softened and contain the scribbles of my thoughts. The cover has scuff marks from being thrown in my bag and shlepped to the beach. The shape has changed from being held in my hands. A book is a companion.

I pour a nip of whisky into my tin camp mug that says *The Good Things In Life.* I then open the faded blue cover of *Eragon* and get lost in Alagaësia, the world of dragons, and the world of words. I know why I'm doing this—because to not would go against who I've always been.

Soul at Rest

Skeleton with a drawn out bow,
Aims down his sight,
Unknowing foe;
A thought that's often
Locked away
Till Grim has taken our last day.

A question stored in stars and sky,
What's our purpose,
Reason why;
It takes a lifetime to uncover
Though only one day to discover.

We all dance to the song of fate,
Don't get so down,
Just grab a date;
'Cause this could be the final song

So live with fire,
Prove me wrong.

Our time on Earth's
No guarantee,
Don't take it lightly,
Here's the key;
Live every day with a full heart,
Your legacy, a lasting art.

'Cause any day could be the last,
So let it go, forget the past;

So when Grim's arrow
Hits our chest,
We'll sleep easy,
Soul at rest.

8
THE LEGACY OF HUMANKIND

RTIST'S POINT IS CONSIDERED ONE OF THE BEST
vistas in Yosemite. It's a lookout above the famous Tunnel View,
where Ansel Adams took his dramatic black and white photography of
Yosemite Valley. I get up extra early, hoping I can watch the sunrise from
Artist's Point. The world remains dark outside of the big sliding window
in my room. I get out of bed and begin my morning routine by draping
the comforter on the floor. I open the window to let in the fresh, cold
air, and then lay down to stretch for a few minutes. It looks like it will be
about a twenty-minute drive from where I'm staying to the Tunnel
View, so I plan on leaving at around 6:30 a.m.

I make a pot of coffee and appreciate the smell of rich, slightly burnt
beans as it fills the room. A simple cup of coffee signifies the beginning
of movement, whether mental or physical. It means something worth
pursuing lays ahead. The gurgling sound of the machine running

through its final motions is symphonic. With the black coffee in my mug, I gear up for my first full day in Yosemite. I throw my bag over my shoulder and step into the icy morning air.

My car is freezing. The back pillow I've been using is as hard as a rock. This is why I'm here: to get up before the sun rises, to watch the entire valley come alive. I'm genuinely excited to experience life; that's what drives me to get up early in the morning. But sometimes I'm afraid. I don't feel ready to face the day. Five minutes turns into ten, then thirty, and then two hours. The inner dialogue begins—*Get up; what are you afraid of?* I'll just lay there, unmoving, although my mind won't stop. I haven't been able to sleep in since high school, even though sometimes all I want to do is rest.

I turn on the engine and warm up the car. The dashboard lights come alive; it feels like getting in my dad's car as a kid. I didn't know what the sound of the blinker was, but it put me to sleep in the backseat. *Tick. Tick. Tick. Tick.* The light of the arrow would blink orange, and I'd drift away. I put the car in reverse and back out of the complex. The car warms as I put on music. *It's going to be a good day.*

I weave along the two-lane road into the valley. As I exit the tunnel, the valley unravels before me. Yosemite Valley is one of those sights that makes one think: *I'm really on Planet Earth,* a rock of a magnificent magnitude. I pull into the empty parking lot and park the car, unable to believe my eyes. On the left is the sheer rock face of El Capitan, cloaked in the soft lavender shade of the early morning. Half Dome and Bridalveil Fall make up the other notable landmarks of the valley.

These are some of the most inspiring natural formations on the face of the Earth, and I am watching the sunrise warm them as it does me.

Looking at them makes me feel small, yet powerful. That's what nature does; that's why it's so beneficial to our psyche. We are small compared to the natural world, yet we have the world within us. I knew this sight was coming when I entered the tunnel, but one can't exactly prepare for this. What would it be like for our ancestors thousands of years ago to come across the sight of Yosemite Valley—to look upon a precipitous rock face and feel a sense of wonder? From where did they see this sight? Maybe from what is now Artist's Point, as they traversed the side of the mountain seeking food, shelter, anything to sustain their lives.

In his book *Sapiens: A Brief History of Humankind*,[18] Israeli historian and author Yuval Noah Harari writes that the Cognitive Revolution occurred between 70,000 and 30,000 years ago. This evolution of the brain gave humans the ability to communicate like never before, think about the future and the past, colonize unknown lands, and devise imaginary realms. Homo Sapiens began drawing cave paintings to depict the magic in the world. If it existed then, perhaps it still exists now. A morning like this makes me believe it does.

I watch the sun rising over Half Dome, a formation of the Earth that has shifted through time and seems as if some extraterrestrial being sliced through the rock like a knife through hot butter. To bear witness to the phenomena of the world in flux is what it means to be alive, back in touch with that part of being that survives and *sees* the beauty for what it is on the surface. This sort of existence, I imagine, would establish pre-Cognitive Revolution Sapiens. But in another sense, connecting with that primordial wonder is to *perceive* something so awe-inspiring, it gives me a reason to believe that there's much more to our existence than only what we see. With nobody around, I gaze upon the dark Earth and let my mind wander.

WITH MY BACKPACK AND CAMERA in tow, I leave the parking lot and begin hiking to Artist's Point. The wooden, weather-beaten signs have eroded and I don't quite know what I'm looking for. A series of stone steps appear, and they beckon. I want to get a better view of when the sun crests over the mountains and illuminates the expanding valley. The moon still shines in the purple sky, like the tail of a bunny in a sea of pale lilacs.

I trudge through thickets of brush and take deep inhalations of the pure morning air. When I pass the sign that reads *Now entering the Yosemite Wilderness,* I consider what I will do if I see a bear. Scream. Get big. After a few miles hiking under the moon, I find a turnout spot I imagine is Artist's Point. There aren't any signs, but the view is incredible, so I throw down my bag and lay down on a smooth granite rock. I watch the sun continue to rise and feel totally at peace. The entire valley is still. I take out my journal and try to write. My hands are stiff and I can barely get more than a few sentences down. That's all I need.

It is me and my mind out here on the side of a mountain, witnessing the simple act of the sun rising over a valley. I think about the conversations I've had and my reason for doing this. I tell myself it is for this or that reason; that I needed to leave home to be alone, and that I needed to go out into the world to write. But what if I just wanted to sit on the side of a mountain and watch the sunrise? There doesn't have to be a reason. There doesn't need to be some revelation or a lightbulb idea that

I'll come home with. I have everything—the world—right before my eyes.

I leave Artist's Point once the sun floats high in the sky. I can sense the changing season down in the valley below. The air is crispy and sweet, yet there isn't snow on the ground. I observe the transitioning season as the golden leaves fall nimbly from the trees above and the branches become bare. There are people in the park, much less than usual during this time of year, but enough to feel like I'm not alone. As we pass, I can sense that they are in awe of this special time. The season turns and the world drifts into a restful sleep.

These formations, this life, this Earth; it's been here forever, forming, changing, building, and falling with time. The seasons continuously keep life exciting and beautiful. I enjoy summer, when we let go and enjoy long days and warm nights around fires and good company. I treasure the fall, when the leaves change and the world cools and the air attains a richness. In the winter, I find peace and comfort in family and friends as the world freezes over. In spring, I cherish the days as life reawakens and we start afresh. Each season has its purpose, just like the seasons of our lives.

As the seconds of the day fall away, I lose myself in the tranquility and grandeur of the valley. It is a day unlike any other. I stay in the valley from dawn until dusk. In the evening, I take a long walk around the valley's base and end up in the middle of Mirror Lake. The lake is empty, so I sit on the vast sandy bottom, usually covered by the crystal clear water from the mountains. I sit beside a teepee structure built of sticks and wood that looks like a bonfire waiting to ignite. To my right, I stare up at the face of Half Dome. A shadow covers half of it; night begins its descent upon the valley.

I can't look away from the mountain. Leaves fall from the trees surrounding the lake, slowly, when nudged by a gust of wind. Nobody but me might see them fall; nobody will hear them crumble or see them fade into the earth. And then one day the full trees will be bare, and we will know winter has come. I honor this moment to slow down with nothing to do but be. I take out my journal and sketch the view of the mountain and the trees surrounding the lake. The colors of the leaves are amber and dark green. I sit in the sand and watch them fall.

TUNNEL VIEW AT DAWN; YOSEMITE VALLEY, CA

LEAVES: FOUR-AND-A-HALF BILLION YEARS in the making. *Four-and-a-half billion years.* That is the age of Planet Earth, of rising and falling seas, global freezing and melting, unfathomable processes and eruptions. How, after all that this planet has endured, have we been able to continue? Why are we here? Why us? And why now? Bill Bryson writes in *A Short History of Nearly Everything*:[19]

> *Not one of your pertinent ancestors was squashed, devoured, drowned, starved, stranded, stuck fast, untimely wounded, or otherwise deflected from its life's quest of delivering a tiny charge of genetic material to the right partner at the right moment in order to perpetuate the only possible sequence of hereditary combinations that could result—eventually, astoundingly, and all too briefly—in you.*

A day can often feel like eternity. A night, gone in the blink of an eye. That's what we are, a flicker of ingenuity in the grand scheme of Earth's history. In retrospect, an entire epoch like the Mesozoic Era when dinosaurs roamed these very lands becomes nothing more than a footnote in a history book. Is that what we might become someday in the distant—or not-so-distant—future? Merely a dash on a timeline in the history of the solar system, half-heartedly glanced at by some extraterrestrial adolescent? *Planet Earth—sounds weird. Next page.* This is assuming some future alien school kid would be turning the pages of a book. *Anyway*—perhaps! If we don't preserve this rock we call home.

We live in what many geologists, ecologists, and other experts refer to as the Anthropocene—*Anthropos* being Greek for human, defined by the impact of human activity on the planet. Erle C. Ellis, Professor of Geography and Environmental Systems at the University of Maryland writes in his book *Anthropocene: A Very Short Introduction:*[20]

> *Overwhelming evidence now confirms that humans are chang-*
> *ing Earth in unprecedented ways. Global climate change, acidi-*
> *fying oceans, shifting global cycles of carbon, nitrogen, and other*
> *elements, forests and other natural habitats transformed into*
> *farms and cities, widespread pollution, radioactive fallout, plas-*
> *tic accumulation, the course of rivers altered, mass extinction of*
> *species, human transport and introduction of species around the*
> *world. These are just some of the many human-induced global*
> *environmental changes that will most likely leave a lasting*
> *record in rock: the basis for marking new intervals of geologic*
> *time.*

For as long as the planet has endured, humans have been more or less a sideshow to the central act, that of nature and its processes. According to the Darwinian theory of evolution, we are just another animal, and the latest on the scene, at that. Yet when we look back at our impact in the radically short amount of time we've been here, it's clear that we're not just another animal. Ellis writes:

Even among the scientific thinkers of Darwin's time, another view was emerging. Humans were not just another primate, but a profoundly disruptive force like no other on Earth.

Various start dates for the Anthropocene have been proposed, ranging from the beginning of the Agricultural Revolution around twelve thousand years ago, up to the mid-twentieth-century and what is known as the Great Acceleration. According to Ellis:

Data conducted in the report Global Change and the Earth System: A Planet Under Pressure shows a dramatic jump in the rate of human and environmental changes starting in the middle of the twentieth-century . . . While acknowledging that human alterations began long ago, the Great Acceleration asserts that human alterations of environments prior to the twentieth-century, though significant in some regions, remained 'well within the bounds of the natural variability of the environment' at global scales. The Anthropocene began not with the rise of agriculture or even the Industrial Revolution, but only with the rise of large-scale industrial societies after 1945 and their unprecedented capacities to alter Earth's environments globally at an accelerating pace.

It's one thing to read the facts regarding the effects of human activity. To read about them can make us feel powerless, as if these problems are too abstract for everyday citizens to have any impact. Yet, it's another to bear witness to the change. Within a lifetime, one might notice the fluctuating smog in a city like Los Angeles, my hometown. I haven't been alive long enough to notice any perceptible change. Until now.

According to an article in the US National Library of Medicine National Institutes of Health, there has been a reduction in greenhouse gases and water pollution in developing countries like India and Bangladesh, as well as ecological restoration in major global tourist spots because of the pandemic.[21] The article states:

> *Due to pollution reduction recently returning of dolphins was reported in the coast of Bay of Bengal (Bangladesh) and canals, waterways, and ports of Venice (Italy) after a long decade.*

AS I SIT IN THE MIDDLE OF THE LAKE, I wonder what this moment would be like on a normal day. *Normal.* What is normal? A year ago, when the park would bustle like Disneyland? Or is three hundred years ago normal, before the Industrial Revolution, or more applicably, the recent Digital Revolution? I hear birds chirping faintly in the distant trees, then, nothing but the sound of silence. Is it possible to return to a time of pristine nature such as the momentary one it feels like I'm in? Ellis writes:

Arrows of Youth

Even as the results of ecological science have helped to characterize the Anthropocene, ecology as a discipline has been reshaped by the need for new approaches to address the ecology of an Earth transformed by human societies. New paradigms have emerged, redefining the value of nature and the role of humans in shaping and curating the ecology of an increasingly anthropogenic biosphere.

Before the pandemic, a classic approach to combat our withering biodiversity would be conservation and restoration to maintain or restore populations and habitats to their natural states, measured by a historical baseline. But then something happened. Life—human life—stopped moving at its normal pace. People could see stars in once devastatingly opaque skies. Stars that told us it is possible to create change, if only to create a world worth living in, where we can harmoniously coexist with this planet. For thousands of years, we simply didn't have the luxury to worry about global ecological preservation when all an individual could think of was finding food to live one more day. Since the emergence of humankind, we've done what we deemed necessary for survival. Yuval Noah Harari writes in *Homo Deus: A Brief History of Tomorrow*:[22]

The same three problems preoccupied the people of twentieth-century China, of medieval India and of ancient Egypt. Famine, plague and war were always at the top of the list.

100

All that governments and kingdoms had time to focus on were the coming wars and preparing for an inevitable plague. Now, these issues are relatively under control compared to the broad historical perspective. We must think bigger.

> *We know quite well what needs to be done in order to prevent famine, plague and war—and we usually succeed in doing it. If we are indeed bringing famine, plague and war under control, what will replace them at the top of the human agenda?*

It's up to us to write the history of our epoch. Will it be a positive one or a disastrous one? Perhaps the pandemic is exactly what we needed to wake up to the possibility that we can indeed be a force for good, down to every individual, through daily acts of consciousness. It will take more than just our individual efforts, but the cooperation of governments and global organizations. But it is possible. Ellis writes:

> *There is a long list of societal actions that have staved off environmental disasters, from the banning of DDT and other pollutants, to laws protecting endangered wildlife that have helped bring species back from the brink of extinction. The rise of parks and protected areas, accelerating investments in carbon-neutral energy systems and technologies from solar energy to electric cars, and growth in consumer-driven environmental protections from 'certified sustainable seafood' labelling to 'LEED certified' energy and resource efficient buildings, all raise the prospect of a better planetary future.*

We've seen the results of global unity regarding the eradication of this virus. It's going to take that same cooperation to reverse the effects we're having on our planet. I will make it my duty to remember this moment when the Earth felt still. We must think about a future that surpasses the lifetime of human beings. We must think about a future past our own life. While humankind may be gone in some distant, or not so distant future, this planet is resilient. But it shouldn't have to work so hard just to be.

Arrows of Youth

Constellations

As the daylight dims,
The stars come out, I can clearly see
Constellations.
Connections of light, perceptible bonds,
Crafted by imagination,
Innate within us all.
The path from one star to another,
Light years apart,
No distance too great to find
Meaning from the human heart.
Through all of time the stars have shone,
Their way through empty darkness;
Beacons of hope,
Guides to brave women and men,
Gods to mortals,
Seeking answers still not found since then.
Forever the way home,
Back to Earth,
Return to self, a grounding glow,
Gone before we see them burn.

9
YOSEMITE FALLS

TODAY'S MISSION: REACH THE TOP OF YOSEMITE Falls. I have an eight-mile round-trip hike in store. I plan to take it slow and draw the day out. The temperature is ideal and the sky is bare of clouds. I go through my morning routine: coffee (I've now bought my own), stretching, and reading *The World Is My Home.* I then make my way down to the valley. The subtle heat of the oncoming day increases as the morning sun sheds its light upon the surrounding mountain faces. I walk to the base of the hike, strengthened by the clean air that pumps through my lungs. The valley glows from the morning light that shines through each falling leaf.

I put in my headphones and listen to the audiobook *Genghis: Birth of an Empire*[23] by Conn Iggulden. It tells the origin story of the twelfth-century Mongolian ruler, Genghis Khan. The first book of the series takes me through the life of Temüjin, the young Khan (emperor) of the

Arrows of Youth

Mongolian Empire. But the young Khan is far from the ruthless conqueror we know him as. He and his brothers are young boys of his father's tribe, known as the Wolves. The Wolves are one of many nomadic tribes that fought like animals on the fierce open plains of Mongolia. When opposing tribe members kill Temüjin's father, the glue holding the Wolves together, the Wolves desert Temüjin and his family; conflicts arise regarding who should assume power. Temüjin, his brothers, and his mother fight for their lives in the barren Mongolian land—the struggle makes them strong and turns Temüjin into a leader. He captures and plunders city after city, expanding throughout Asia and into Eurasia, making him one of the greatest conquerors of all time and the first Great Khan of the now unified Mongolian people.

As I listen to legends of Temüjin and his brothers hiking the craggy and blustery red hills to reach the nest of a rare eagle, I can't help but feel like a wayfarer seeking my own treasured eagle. My goal is intangible. There is something I aspire to discover at the top of the falls; it's the energy that gets me up and out of my bed at the crack of dawn day after day. My eagle is the experience of the unknown. With each step I take, I cultivate a reverence for the natural world deep within my bones. I long to reach the top of that mountain for nothing more than a view to remember.

I'm about halfway up when I realize the perpendicular rock face I'm staring at is where the waterfall usually roars. I smile as I gaze upon the slab of onyx and silver granite basking in the sun. It's no less beautiful, yet the waterfall flows in the late winter and spring, when the mountain snow has had time to melt. I sit on a stone and take out my headphones while I peel an orange. On the other side of the valley sits Half Dome in all of its glory. I find a reason to carry on, if only to look at the astonishing mountain from a higher vantage point. A couple of faint voices coming from the switchbacks below me break the restful silence. They sound like men my age; I feel a connection when they come into view.

"I guess she's not falling!" I profess to them as we exchange words like companions.

"Is that supposed to be it?" one of them asks. He wields a GoPro on a long stick.

"Yeah, that's her; well, it's still beautiful," I reply. They're friends from Duke University in North Carolina and have made the journey to Yosemite from across the country. That fills me up. They are out here for the same reason as me; they're answering the call to adventure. As they continue, I stay for a few more minutes. There is nowhere to rush. I have a day to do nothing but climb a mountain.

THE SCENERY SWIFTLY alters as I near the top. On the climb, the leaves on the trees are golden brown and dark green. Suddenly the mountain scenery becomes saturated by a verdant, bright shade of green. The trees look as if they've been touched by the icy breath of space. Up here they adapt to a distinct atmosphere where the winds are raw and tumultuous. I feel exposed to the elements; the sun feels glorious as it shines down on my skin and warms me to my core. I reach a new level of peaceful solitude as I climb through the sky.

The top of the mountain looks like the otherworldly domain of Mount Olympus, where the gods have been relaxing for millions of years. There are small groups of people spread out having lunch and enjoying the fruits of their strenuous labor. I am the newest addition. I have to look at the waterfall, even though I know it won't be flowing.

I find a way down to the pool where the water usually leaps from the edge of the cliff. I scale a few small rock faces and shimmy down the granite stones to reach a small, reflective pool. I lay down my things on the large, curved, smooth stone. The lads are sitting by the water's edge; we have something in common, perhaps that we are young and seek the excitement in life. Reaching the top wasn't the end of the journey. They found their way to the pool, and I commend them.

I lay down and listen to the water turn from bank to bank, pool to pool. The water is still moving, although there isn't enough force to create the actual waterfall. It is better this way; I can get close to the water without fearing being swept away. I sit close to the pool's edge, dip my bandana into the icy clear water, and press it to my face. Then I shut my eyes and listen. There are different levels to the sounds of moving water; in front of where I sit, the flowing stream banks and glides into a large pool. The gentle, repeating sound puts my mind at ease. It's the unceasing voice, the heartbeat, the life of the planet. I think about where the sound originates. The water drops into the small pools and makes a dunking sound, but is there sound from the gliding of water against stone?

In a couple of hours, human beings can climb and explore the planet with nothing but our will and two feet. This has always baffled and excited me. Humans throughout history have marched from country to country to fight for the land they believed they were due. While I can't understand the need to conquer, I can't help but wonder what it must have been like to be a part of one of those grueling campaigns.

One that is utterly staggering comes from the Punic Wars between the cities of Carthage and Rome, the two leading powers of the western Mediterranean in the third century BC. In 218 BC, Hannibal, the military general of the Phoenician city of Carthage (modern-day Tunisia), essentially circled the entire Mediterranean Sea by land, crossing the Pyrenees and the Alps by elephant to reach and lay waste to the Roman Republic.[24] As battles raged between the Roman Republic and the Carthaginians over the next several decades, the Roman senator Cato became famous for ending every speech he made, no matter the subject, with the line: "And furthermore, my opinion is that Carthage should be destroyed—*delendam esse Carthaginem.*" The Romans put this advice to use, and in 146 BC, the Third Punic War came to an end with the total defeat of Carthage and the destruction of the city.

What drove these possessed generals to do anything to assure their names would populate the history books? Julius Caesar, Hannibal, Napoleon, Genghis Khan—more land, wealth, and death never satisfied them. Once they tasted the blood of their enemies, they only sought more until they drove their people to the ends of the Earth. I'm just thankful to be alive today.

MY BODY FEELS vigorously conscious from the climb. Out here amid nature, my mind and spirit feel united with my body. This single entity has brought me to where I sit, overlooking the highest waterfall in North America. Today, the water can't find the nerve to leap. I want to spend the entire day sitting here, listening to the Earth. I look beyond the opening in the rock face where the water usually leaves the mountain, and gaze across the valley.

It's just me, alone under the sun, a body on a rock, a rock atop another rock, floating in endless space. I feel something within, as if I possess the energy of the sun. I study my reflection in the placid pool of water beside me. We contain so much—an individual history and a world to explore. Yet we still limit our human capacity. Our mind expands as far as the edges of the solar system, yet often it feels like it's in a cage. I could step off the ledge and fly.

The sun has begun its descent to rise in another land, and I too have to begin my way down. I notice there aren't many people left—in fact, nobody at all. For a moment, worry overwhelms me; perhaps I shouldn't be here by myself. I panic and begin bulldozing through brush and pines, anxiously searching for the path back down that seems to have disappeared. I'm breaking branches and forcing my way until I come to a ledge, not off of the face of the cliff, but about fifteen feet high. *Can't do that.* I have to climb back up through the bushes until I eventually find a route, albeit not a clear one, that will bring me to the distant path I see. *How did this happen?*

I work my way through until I come to a smaller, manageable ledge. I made it back to the path and stand there for a moment, feeling safe once again. Two girls in conversation pass. I stand on the ledge overhead, dirty and covered in pine needles from my detour. I have to say something or this will look strange.

"Barreling through the bushes is never a good idea!" I call out with a smile. They laugh and look up, slightly amused, or finding me odd. Either way, I'm okay. I hop down and begin my slow descent. The path darkens with every step. I focus on each stone—*One at a time, enjoy the journey, dismiss thoughts of reaching the bottom.*

Half Dome looks as if dipped in a hazy golden shell. I stop to listen to the rustling leaves as a pleasant wind blows through the valley. It reminds me of the tranquility I found in Japan exactly a year ago, listening to the trees. I'm touched by a sense of sweet serenity. Darkness slowly envelopes the landscape: the snowy mountains far beyond Half Dome, the forest of evergreen trees down below, and Half Dome—the marvel of this inspiring cradle of Earth. Daylight leaves the valley and I walk to my car in the dark. I'm fulfilled, inspired, and full of joy. I've come down the mountain with my own rare eagle—the lasting memory of the falls that wouldn't fall. Tomorrow, I leave for the Redwood Forests of Northern California.

Arrows of Youth

THE TOP OF YOSEMITE FALLS

Morning Moon

The light is not yet here,
Beginning a new day,
Illuminating our existence and who we will be.
There is still time to hide,
To stay under,
To wonder.

The moon in the place of the sun
Lights the way for the morning traveler,
Still foggy as the coastline which they wander,
The horizon awash as the rest of the Earth,
Hazy like blue charcoal,
Slowly more definite as the moon makes its landing.

Down here life moves,
Up there, silence.
It paves the way of our dreams.

10
SEEDS OF JOY

YOSEMITE IS KNOWN FOR ITS GIANT SEQUOIAS, or "Sierra Redwoods." The true Redwoods, however, exist only within the foggy, dense, and salty belt of the Northern California Coast between Big Sur and Southwestern Oregon. The salt in the air emanates from the sea and infuses with the soil. This breathes vitality into the Northern California forests. I'm ready to leave the mountains and get lost amongst them. I plan on staying in Trinidad, a coastal town nestled within the towering trees about ninety minutes from the Oregon border. It seems like an ideal launching point to access the different Redwood National Parks which populate California's relatively obscure northern pocket. On paper, the drive from Yosemite to Trinidad should take about six hours.

It takes approximately two hours to get off the mountain and into the California agricultural heartland. I don't know if I'm driving in circles or if the mountain air is destroying my capacity to think, but at a certain point I question if I've seen the same pasture three times. I'm numb from hours behind the wheel. As I drift along the two-lane highway through the California haze, I think about how my life is changing.

All I must do is accelerate, turn, and brake—movements that have become second nature after years. The day passes like an old, grainy film. I drive speedily along the highway where a single road extends for miles into the horizon and undulates like a roller coaster through waves of golden brown fields as far as I can see.

I stop to glance around at train crossings and get out of the car from time to time and take pictures. I take the pressure off of myself when driving these long distances; there's no rush. I enjoy exploring the distinct cities and pastoral interior of my home state. This agricultural landscape is scattered with grim black trees reminiscent of scenes described by the twentieth-century author John Steinbeck. He called this land *East of Eden*.[25] As I drive and gaze upon distant horizons, I lose myself in Steinbeck's tale that weaves with this barren Earth. I pass a general store advertising a tequila bar and cold beer. I smile at the jerky stands that look like originals from the nineteenth-century California Gold Rush.

I see signs for King City, a place I've regarded as not much more than a pit stop between Northern and Southern California. After reading *East of Eden*, I'm intrigued by these cultural hubs of the early twentieth century. According to Steinbeck, anybody who wanted them would receive acres of land, even if the land was unworkable. After coming from the East Coast's dense cities, people couldn't believe they could get so much for so little. As I pass the endless fields, I can imagine the freedom they must have felt. The more I see of this vast rural state, the more I appreciate its history and unique scenery. Steinbeck's scenes and characters and endearing moments have stayed with me.

A powerful story becomes a part of you and blends realities; I look out into the boundless fields and envision *East of Eden*. In the book, the characters struggle to remain moral when regularly tempted to be otherwise. Our consciousness is our constant companion; to keep it clear takes doing what isn't always easy, but what feels intrinsically right in our heart and soul. Perhaps this is something we're born with, an inner moral compass that will guide us to a virtuous life if left alone. But it's not left alone.

The characters in the story long to be decent, yet they're human beings with faults that arise from living on this Earth. The book encompasses many parallels with the Old Testament book of Genesis, especially the story of Cain and Abel. Steinbeck based the principal characters, Cal and Aron Trask, on the biblical brothers. Cal, based on Cain, wants more than anything to be noble, yet he can't seem to change his ways. Aron studies to become a priest, a leader among people, similar to a shepherd leading sheep. He's compared to Abel, a *"keeper of sheep"* (Gen. 4:2).[26] According to Steinbeck, *East of Eden* was his masterpiece, the story he had always wanted to write. Steinbeck wrote to a friend after completing his manuscript:

I finished my book a week ago. [. . .] Much the longest and sure-
ly the most difficult work I have ever done . . . I have put all the
things I have wanted to write all my life. This is 'the book.' If it
is not good I have fooled myself all the time. I don't mean I will
stop but this is a definite milestone and I feel released. Having
done this I can do anything I want. Always I had this book
waiting to be written.[27]

Day in and day out, being human tests our moral compass. It's a daily challenge to keep our hands clean and our hearts pure. This life is a battle, one worth fighting indefatigably for what we know is right. *East of Eden* is a story of redemption, for no day is a wasted opportunity to be who we long to be. As a reader, I felt like I grew with the brothers and could feel for them, not only seeing them for their mistakes, but their desire to change. Excellent writing provides this human connection.

We don't love characters who are perfect, as they're difficult to relate to. The best characters in stories grow and evolve; we too change as readers and see why they may do what they do. It's only human to fall to temptation. Yet like the characters in the story who are genuinely good inside and desire to get better, we all deserve a chance at redemption. Steinbeck brilliantly conveys the struggle to be human and to question what is right and wrong. According to the renowned psychologist Jordan Peterson, this is the study of ethics. He writes in his transformative book *12 Rules for Life*:[28]

The philosophical study of right and wrong is ethics. Even older and deeper than ethics is religion. Religion concerns itself not with (mere) right and wrong but with good and evil themselves. Religion concerns itself with the domain of value, ultimate value. That is not the scientific domain. The people who wrote and edited the Bible, for example, weren't scientists. They couldn't have been scientists, even if they had wanted to be. The viewpoints, methods and practices of science hadn't been formulated when the Bible was written. Religion is instead about proper behavior. A genuine religious acolyte isn't trying to formulate accurate ideas about the objective nature of the world. He's striving, instead, to be a 'good person.'

Steinbeck uses the deeply rooted themes of the Bible to depict the inner turmoil of questioning who we are, what we're becoming, and what it means to go against the norm. It's challenging to know what is truly right or wrong; society tells us one thing, but we feel in our inner depths the call of our individual truth. We have to make the conscious decision to act according to this truth. We're born with it, yet who we are becomes complicated as we become integrated into society.

We want what others have because we think that will bring us joy. We compare ourselves to others because we believe they've reached a level of success that we are due. But that means we're then seeking joy from the world instead of from within. We become frustrated about what we want—is it what we *should* want, or what we truly want? If our actions don't align with our values, there will always be the voice within us that says *This isn't you.*

It's not until we live our own truth that the inner voice will quiet. We must go inward. This will provide the adventure of a lifetime. When we go in, we become magnetic to all living things. We can then stop looking and just *see*. When we find joy in ourselves and in who we are, we can perceive the true nature of existence. We see life for what it is, what it's always been, a place without labels and self-imposed fear. *The only way out is to go in.* Maybe Steinbeck knew this.

He felt this story was his calling in life, to decipher the Bible—a fluid, cryptic text—in a relatable way. *East of Eden* makes me think deeply about my own beliefs of right and wrong, good and bad. I believe being good in the world provides the individual with meaning. This doesn't mean just seeking out ways to be good (although we very well may), but doing what's good in every adventure we embark on. Perhaps to be good is to see ourselves in one another. We may all realize that we are capable, if seen through eyes of love instead of hate, as we see the world as a reflection of what we feel inside, to be who we truly are—good.

THE TRUE HERO OF THE STORY IS LEE, the philosophical companion to Adam Trask, Cal and Aron's father. Lee's dream is to leave the ranch he's worked on for his entire life and head to San Francisco to open up a bookstore. This, he believes, will finally bring him inner joy. But he eventually returns to the ranch, realizing it wasn't something in the exterior world he had to change. He chased his illusory dream, but in reality, he had everything he ever wanted on that ranch: a family. That gave him more meaning than his bookstore. But he had to try. If he didn't, he would always have wondered.

As I drive from Fresno to San Francisco, I feel like I'm making a historic drive reminiscent of *East of Eden*. On a trip like this, the drive is just as much part of the journey as the destination. Still, I come to understand that the drive is going to take about eleven hours total to get to the Redwoods. I decide to stop in San Francisco to have dinner with a few of my best friends.

I love San Francisco. If I can stop while passing by, I will. As a kid from Los Angeles, I always imagined it as the great city of the north, characterized by rain and football. The first time I went to San Francisco was with Morgan and my dad for a Raiders versus Lions football game. The six-hour drive felt endless as a sixth grader. We drove all day (or so I thought) and into the night before reaching the inclement city. In San Francisco, life meant dark and early mornings with hot coffee and the musk of the wharf. It meant sunny afternoons eating clam chowder and listening to squawking seagulls. It meant evenings of watching football bundled up in big jackets and thick beanies. The game was intensely rowdy. It turned absurd for Morgan, who had a three-hundred-pound Raiders fan barking in his ear the entire game.

"SUH! SUH! YOU'RE GARBAGE! SUH!!!" Ndamukong Suh was a player on the Lions. I felt terrible for Mo, who still enjoyed the game despite the unruly fan. My dad made us leave about ten minutes before the game ended to beat the mad rush of fans out of the stadium. We tried to outsmart the system and welcomed our fate. The game finished in stellar fashion. All we could hear were cries of Raider triumph radiating from the stadium as we walked in the cold on the outskirts of the parking lot. I foster the same love now as I did then for the grungy, classic, beautiful city of hills that is San Francisco. Life derives meaning when experienced with the ones we love. Embracing the cold and a long drive up to San Francisco with my dad and best friend is a memory I'll always have, an *arrow of youth*. I didn't know it then. But if it brings me this much joy to think about it now, I don't think it matters. Perhaps that's what memories are: seeds of joy to plant for our future self to harvest.

WHEN ON THE ROAD I hear my dad's voice saying "no have-to's!" forever in the back of my mind. This motto served as the backbone of many childhood journeys and continues to pilot my trips today. It means nobody has to do anything they don't want to do.

To have traveled as much as I have with my dad is a blessing. As a kid on trips together, it didn't matter where we were; we'd always visit the local park or tennis courts. If possible, we'd take a dip in the ocean as the day's first event. I was young and often grumpy and would have rather stayed in the hotel room. But I'm grateful my dad always encouraged me to come with a coffee in hand and a smile on his face. He planted a seed in my character not to seek what was easy, but to get up and at 'em to take advantage of my time on this Earth.

The happiness that makes life worth living doesn't come from the things we can buy. It comes from the moments we can appreciate, the ones the pandemic has given us a second chance to cherish. To me, happiness comes from running through a small charming town and watching night turn into day. Happiness comes when walking in awe below the towering skyscrapers of a modern metropolis. It comes from the repetitive satisfaction of hitting tennis balls against a wood backboard— clearly something passed down. More relevant, as I've spent time in

Malibu during the pandemic, are the beach walks I've taken with my dad in the rain. I don't know what can top that, no matter where we are.

My dad wanted Morgan and I to share that experience because he wanted to make us happy; still, we left early. My dad has shown my brothers and me through his actions that the freedoms such as getting on the road with nothing but a map and a head full of thoughts are the good things in life. Nobody can take them away. That's how his father Dicky lived, and my great-grandfather, also named Dick, before him. When I jump in the ocean and feel the ice-cold water rejuvenate my spirit, I think not only of my dad. I think of my entire family as we together share this passion for living. This trait is in our DNA; the cold ocean water is in our blood.

Like planting a seed in the sodden earth—of fruit to nourish others, of flowers to lend beauty to the world, of a tree which will one day be strong and provide shade to the weary—we must live to plant seeds of joy. To share the gift of life and the healing that the Earth brings is to impart a piece of our soul, the only part of us which eternally remains. Every experience with friends, every time we lend a hand expecting nothing in return, every time we smile to an unknowing stranger, we're planting seeds of joy.

I can't imagine the love a parent feels for their child, as I'm far from having any kids of my own. But I have been a brother for twenty-five years; I've been a grandson, and I've been a son. I cherish my parents and what they've given me—an ideal to strive towards. My dad is a human being with faults like the rest of us. Nobody's perfect, and perfection isn't my goal. My dad is the man I aim to be, full of heart and spirit and adventure. I think of him always; a man who follows his inner compass, a man who strives to be good.

I arrive at Pete, Ramin, and Luke's apartment at around 6:00 p.m. We go to a ramen shop on the corner to boost our morale. The kind woman who runs the shop gives us a corner table outside.

"We're told restaurants are shutting down in a week, so I didn't re-open!" It seems she's told this story before. I want to know how she feels. "But then they don't shut down and we don't know what to do. And then when we re-open, they shut down!" She explains the difficulties restaurants have been facing during the pandemic. If running a restaurant wasn't the most demanding job on the planet before, the pandemic raised the stakes. Like many small business owners fighting to stay alive, she has persevered and stayed afloat by genuinely caring about her community.

She places cold mugs of beer on the small, teetering corner table. We're huddled around, feeding off each other's warmth and excited conversation. The bubbles rise from the bottom of the rich brew and create a lovely foam top. We cheer the pints—to us, to her, to getting through this time together. Her smile and laughter tell me she's never going to give in.

"Gentlemen," I hug the boys back in the warmth of their apartment. It's tough to leave, I consider staying the night. No; I'll see them soon and have to pull myself away. "I will see you all on my way back!" The luminous streets of San Francisco hold a special place in my heart. The road flows downhill like a stream straight into the bay. I follow the lights and leave the boys, ready to get lost amongst the world's tallest trees.

EAST

OF EDEN

Essence of You

After navigating stormy seas,
Safe harbor always to return,
Where you mustn't hide
Behind self-built walls,
But only act, think, be, as you.

Life will blow you
Every which way,
Tempt and try,
Allure and mystify,
Sometimes, you feel you
Have no say.

You need the space to think about,
What truly makes you, you,
Break through the noise control,
The barrier of thought and truth.

Instead of speaking
Heartfelt words,
The artist's tongue,
Explorer's vision,
Your circumstances
Have more sway.

To get there past the
Point of no return,
You take a stand, line in the sand,
To live and learn,
To learn and live.

One is reactive,
One is purposeful,
Perhaps you need them both,
To find what makes you, you.

11

INTO THE FOREST

A THREE-QUARTER MOON LIGHTS UP the foggy sky like a shimmering yellow stone floating below the crest of a dark, opaque sea. I drive along the serpentine highway that weaves through the dense evergreen forests of Northern California. A soft rain falls upon my windshield. I settle in. I turn my high beams on as a grey fog permeates the route. The headlights illuminate the misty forest and the night sky. Cars project on the side of the mountain, or is it a hill? I can't be sure in the dark. The shadows of cars grow as they near, like monsters of a dream. It provides a bit of comfort when I pass other cars in the ominous night. I turn on an episode of the *Tim Ferris Podcast*[29] where Tim interviews the aforementioned historian and author Yuval Noah Harari.

Harari's books *Sapiens*, *Homo Deus*, and *21 Lessons for the 21st Century*[30] tell the story of human history from the beginning while exploring where we're headed in our next phase of existence, if there will be one. In *Homo Deus*, Harari expounds on humanism, a concept that has captivated me the more I strive to develop a harmonious sense of being with myself and the world around me. The belief in humanism upholds an acceptance of any religion or perspective as long as it causes nobody else harm. It maintains the notion that there is no objective divine presence that controls our lives. Rather, our fate is in our own hands; what we connect with inside of us creates our meaning.

No person or religion is more "correct" than the other. But that doesn't mean there isn't some greater good, some higher power in which to place one's faith. Perhaps it is God. But God is just a word we've used to label this unexplainable presence. I believe God is whatever makes one live their best life, aimed to achieve the highest good for all. God may be nature; it may be a figure up above. God is within, and that creates our God without.

If your God brings you inner peace and helps you be in the best relationship with existence, then I believe in it, too. But my God may be something different. I'm still uncovering what it is, but I acknowledge there's something greater. It's the energy I find in people and all things; the beauty of the cosmos within a single stone.

We don't all have to be the same. If we were, this life would be incredibly uninteresting. I heard it said by the inspiring Dr. Zach Bush that there's a difference between conformity and unity.[31] Dr. Bush is a physician dedicated to the health of humanity and the planet, specializing in internal medicine, endocrinology, and hospice care. Unity means honoring each other's differences and creating a bond where both parties strive to live amongst one another in peace. We have the choice to foster this mentality as a planet; too often we choose not to. Conformity means *you must be like me.* Nobody knows the correct way to live. We're meant to figure it out together, not divided.

BEFORE THE LAST FEW CENTURIES, humans believed they played a part in some great cosmic plan "devised by the omnipotent Gods or the eternal laws of nature," writes Yuval Noah Harari in *Homo Deus.*

> *The cosmic plan gave meaning to human life, but also restricted human power. Humans were much like actors on a stage.*

Because humans put their fate into the hands of the gods, they believed their lives gained meaning in return. According to Harari, if people fought bravely in war, lived their lives according to the rules of their religion, and worked hard to support their king, then they played a role in this cosmic drama. According to humanism, things are different. We can be anything, think anything, and do anything. We can adhere to our inner muse if we have the grit, and if our beliefs harm nobody else.

It isn't the hand of fate that will decide how our lives turn out, but our everyday actions. It isn't God who decides our life's purpose, but the fire within our soul that steers the way. Yet if it were so simple, everybody would follow their hearts in perfect contentment. Understanding, listening, and trusting our inner voice as it connects with the world can be complicated. As the world rapidly changes, it becomes increasingly so.

I believe in God, but to me God isn't a man who sits in his golden throne with a long flowing beard. If nature is your reason for being, if fate is your greatest motivator, if the sun is your almighty lord, then that's what should inspire you. Religion provides structure, an apex to strive for based on lessons formed over thousands of years. Yet as Steinbeck illustrated in *East of Eden,* life, being human and knowing how to trust ourselves is incredibly complex.

There is no right way forward or correct way to live, and that's what makes each of our journeys unlike any other. It's the everyday discovery from the moment we're born until the day we die that makes life an adventure. Still, it's a complicated world. We don't always know how to follow our hearts, as they speak to us in a mosaic of often conflicting ways. Harari writes:

> *Accordingly, the central religious revolution of modernity was not losing faith in God; rather, it was gaining faith in humanity. It took centuries of hard work . . . Humanism has taught us that something can be bad only if it causes somebody to feel bad.*

That's where we've gone wrong throughout history. We've thought as human beings that our way is the best. We've sought to enlighten the rest of the world when they didn't ask for it. If your religion, or anything you do brings you joy and hurts nobody else, then pursue it. This should be the motto of our modern day. The future will always change, but what continues to puzzle me regarding religion is how many archaic practices still retain validity for many people. If these practices cause harm to others, why would we continue to practice them in our modern world?

What was normal yesterday may change when a single soul challenges what's thought of as normal. They challenge their own beliefs and the beliefs of the masses. Somebody dares to be different. Harari discusses the webs of meaning that have been spun since the beginning of time. These are stories we all buy into collectively that aren't necessarily true in themselves, but become real when we place our faith in them.

> *Meaning is created when many people weave together a common network of stories. People constantly enforce each other's beliefs in a self-perpetuating loop. Each round of mutual confirmation tightens the web of meaning further until you have little choice but to believe what everyone else believes. Yet over decades and centuries, the web of meaning unravels and a new web is spun in its place. To study history means to watch the spinning and unraveling of these webs, and to realize that what seems to people in one age the most important thing in life becomes utterly meaningless to their descendants.*

We subconsciously recognize the rules of society placed all around us. We don't see them laid out; rather, we see successful people and want what they have, believing that equates to happiness. But it doesn't. Instead, it's the questioning of the norms and constantly asking: *How does my soul connect to what I'm doing?* That may move us forward as individuals, and as a planet. As Harari says, we derive meaning from the perspective of the masses. Over time, this way of living creates a culture which, whether or not we buy into it, defines our modern age. Harari writes:

> *We take this reality for granted, thinking it is natural, inevitable and immutable. We forget that our world was created by an accidental chain of events, and that history shaped not only our technology, politics and society, but also our thoughts, fears and dreams. We have felt that grip from the moment we were born, so we assume that it is a natural and inescapable part of who we are.*

We must challenge the rules and norms of society that need challenging, as this constant tension between the vanguard of change and the bedrock of society shapes our modern day and ushers us into the future. But there must be openness, discussion, and a genuine desire to want to change for the better. That's what I believe is missing. We've lost the ability to come together in attempting to understand one another. But this paradigm can change any time we decide to listen. As Harari says, we were born into this society and reality. While it's undoubtedly the best time to be alive in terms of safety and possibilities, that doesn't mean our modern-day is perfect. George Orwell writes in his dystopian novel *1984*:[32]

> *Being in a minority, even a minority of one, did not make you mad. There was truth and there was untruth, and if you clung to the truth even against the whole world, you were not mad.*

Winston Smith, the protagonist in the totalitarian world of *1984*, seeks truth in a culture devoid of the idea. But does that mean it isn't there? When the drum of the masses is beating and all signs point forward, does that deem that path true? In the active progression of youth, the way forward is not just in accepting what is, but in challenging what's normal *if* in need of change. This doesn't mean being an anarchist; it means questioning what doesn't seem right. When we observe something about the world or about ourselves we don't like, we can tell ourselves: *It doesn't have to be this way.*

I see this quote from the book as saying: who actually knows what is the *right* way to live? Is there one? We've been attempting to figure this out since the beginning of humankind. Well, what if we start, at a minimum, with human rights—the freedom for all people to do what they desire as long as it's peaceful and helps them live their best life. Let's agree that "freedom" includes the custom to discuss, question, learn from each other, and grow together. This, Jordan Peterson writes in *12 Rules for Life*, is the proper way to live and the only way to coexist in harmony:

The final type of conversation, akin to listening, is a form of mutual exploration. It requires true reciprocity on the part of those listening and speaking. It allows all participants to express and organize their thoughts. A conversation of mutual exploration has a topic, generally complex, of genuine interest to the participants. Everyone participating is trying to solve a problem, instead of insisting on the a priori validity of their own positions. All are acting on the premise that they have something to learn. This kind of conversation constitutes active philosophy, the highest form of thought, and the best preparation for proper living.

The modern world is at our fingertips, literally. It feels acceptable to stare at a small screen for hours on end, because that's become the norm. There's an influx of unnecessary information we accrue that becomes cumbersome in our lives. When you're stripped of the unnecessary noise, what is there left to bear? When there's no more meaning established by society—no more name, profession, likes, family, friends, or preconceived notions, who are you, really? *What would you do if you were the last person on Earth?* It's an insightful question to ponder. Yet, I keep returning to an answer: just be. Your calling to be is your North Star. Follow it. On the way to the Redwoods on a cold and misty night, I'm following my own.

AT AROUND 11:30 P.M., I pull into the driveway. *Whoa, I forgot I'm staying at somebody's house.* This should be interesting. The home has a mystical aura, like a witch's cottage. An ominous feeling returns. *It's fine* I tell myself to quell the thought. I creep over the creaking deck that looks into the kitchen. *I don't want to look, expecting there to be somebody looking back at me.* Snap out of it! *Stay focused.* It's spooky, but part of the adventure. I make my way to the room through a sliding door connected to the deck. There is a garden; I can hear the crickets and the faint, erratic croak of frogs down by the creek. *Listen to the sounds of night.*

The air is damp; I can see the cold clearly outlined with each breath. There's a subtle smell of roses, awakened from the rain. This feels strange—entering a home in the forest in the middle of the night. *It'll be cheerful in the morning*, I tell myself. *Just get under the covers.* Several bugs hover in midair, enamored by the light. *Damn*, I let them in while I opened the door. It could be worse. Much worse. The room has enough space for a bed, a dresser, and a desk. The dresser's empty and has an angelic image of Mother Mary painted on the side. The desk is small and eggshell white. *This isn't so bad.* It could be my grandma's, or sleeping at a distant cousin's I've never met. I pull the comforter to my chin and try to stop thinking. The opposite happens.

I WAKE UP TO Yuval Noah Harari's voice playing in the living room. *No way.* I have to introduce myself. I put my bare feet on the shaggy carpet and walk out into the living room. To my dismay, Yuval Noah Harari is not the homeowner. Rather, the owner of the house is listening to the same podcast that I'd listened to on the drive.

"Good morning," I say, trying not to startle the elderly woman, but loud enough not to be frighteningly quiet, either. She turns to face me from the other side of the room. I do my best to act natural, as if it's not strange that I'm here; we both smile. I hadn't yet seen the rest of the home until now. There are magazines and books strewn around the rustic living room. It's warm inside. There's a fire smoldering in a small fireplace and documents spread out on the main kitchen table.

"I'm Vincent; I'm staying in the guest room. I had to come out here when I heard Yuval Noah Harari! I was listening to this same thing on the way here from San Francisco." I'm genuinely excited about the coincidence.

"Oh, I think he's fascinating," she says. "He's talking about the way humans have spun webs of meaning throughout history."

Indeed. Her son strolls into the room with a couple of cups of steaming hot coffee. He's a quirky young man with the hood of his fuzzy jacket over his head. Fine blonde hair falls in front of his face.

"Good morning," he says with a welcoming smile. He hands his mom and me the mugs; my spirit lifts as my hands warm. We talk about the trip, where I'm heading, and what I plan to do today. Then I take my coffee to the backyard through my room.

The yard is full of budding red and white roses. Smoke rises from the yurt in the corner of the yard where other travelers are staying. It smells like firewood and fresh pine. The rising sun breaks through the tall surrounding trees; it warms my skin and melts the lingering morning dew. I knew the morning would be better.

Where Does He Hide?

Where does he hide,

Underneath this mask of self;

Is it me, striving to amass some wealth?

Flowing from my heart,

My truth—

Dammed is this river red,

Thoughts bury essence, no steady passage,

I ruminate inside my head.

Where does he hide,

A formless being collects no dust,

Bereft of things, with rain they only rot and rust.

The water falls to wash away,

The memories of yesterday,

A boldness which has brought me here,

Look around and then look up,

The path ahead is far from clear.

Does he hide between the swaying trees?

Does he live amongst the stinging bees?

Perhaps he could find a joy like they,

Nomadic life,

Through travels they do seldom stay,
For all that's needed, spirit fostered from within,
To face the world,
Uncover what has always been.
In shallow water, feet wade
Though planted firmly on the ground,
That's not where he hides,
That's not where he's found.
Swimming further in translucent blue,
The sun, its rays,
They reach and pierce
All the way through,
At once I thought I could not see;
My legs, they kick!
Afloat I strive always to be.
Perhaps he's here,
I can't be sure,
For who's to tell the real me?
For now at rest,
A peaceful state,
Floating in the endless sea.

12

THE WORLD'S TALLEST TREES

PRAIRIE CREEK STATE PARK IS ABOUT an hour from Trinidad. I reach the parking lot of the James Irvine Trail and step into the rising sun. I should probably eat before this eleven-mile hike. A peanut butter sandwich sounds tasty, as it's something I never eat at home. Peanut butter is a crucial ingredient of the road trip diet, and I'm not complaining. With my mouth glued shut from a full bite of peanut butter and grainy, sprouted bread, I can barely talk, let alone breathe.

A van pulls up beside me in this inopportune moment. A man who looks about my age comes around to the side of the car I'm leaning on. He has bushy hair stuffed under a flat-billed cap, a thin leather vest over a long wheat-colored shirt, and a smirk that makes me believe we'd be great friends. He moves slowly and points his face towards the sky. I like his vibe.

I want to speak but struggle to get the peanut butter down. A girl sits in the front seat, taking her time as well. I listen to the sound of chirping birds coming from the trees. This couple seems like adventurers, explorers, perhaps Cal Poly alumni by the way they look. *Peanut butter's down.*

"How's it going?" I blurt out with a smile, still lifting peanut butter from the roof of my mouth with my tongue. He looks over, smiling, waiting to strike up a few words.

"Hello. Gorgeous day."

"It is. Are you guys from around here?" I ask while still working on extracting the glue from my mouth.

"No, Oregon. We thought this was a good time for a road trip." This explains a lot. They display the outdoorsy simplicity of those I know from Oregon. I find similarities between myself and those I'm meeting on the road. They don't have to be here; they want to be. What if we could do more of the things that make us happy, truly happy, like spending the day walking through a forest, or getting in the van and seeing the country, or creating something meaningful? I believe we can.

"I'll see you guys out there!"

IF GREEN IS THE COLOR OF LIFE, then the forest is alive. It only takes a few steps into the thicket to realize I've entered something magical. Every deep inhalation of the salty air enhances my perception. I can almost taste the forest flowing from the leaves. I can feel the magnetic pulse of this breathing environment. All I can see is green in every direction; fallen branches and oceans of wood, damp paths and a floating ecosystem. Shadows pervade the forest as if Robin Hood awaits behind some tree for an unknowing nobleman to saunter through the dense brush before lurching out to take his gold. I walk at a clip that I'll have to maintain if I want to reach the ocean before dusk. It's five-and-a-half miles through the red giants. Still, I take the time to stop and marvel at the individual trees, which look as if a dinosaur used them as a back scratch.

Some have what looks like claw marks of a T-Rex; others are petrified, ancient, 2,000 years old. Presumably, many of the trees were infants when Jesus walked the Earth. I walk through the forest and imagine myself as if in a book. *I am.* Life can be fun if we make it so. The air is rich and carries the smell of the briny ocean. The ground feels good to walk on; every step gives; I make my way in long strides. The sheer magnitude of the environment is astounding. I look up at the towering trees, more mystical and uncharted than Mariposa Grove; I feel them smiling down on me. I pass over bridges and meadows and feel like I am a part of something that truly exists—*exists*—*is existing.* Life in the forest doesn't stop. People like me come and go, but the trees don't leave; they grab hold of the earth, so I do, too.

I explore the fallen logs and put my hands in the dirt. My spirit floats high above the tallest trees and soars back down to dance. A single song can carry us through life. Don't let it be a sad one. Let it be a song like those sung since the sirens swum the seas. Make it a song that's full of rhythm and grace. Ensure it's a song to always return and feel a sense of individuality. Let it be a song of you. I don't care if anybody sees me. I lose myself in the best way possible. I am dancing to the beat of my drum, all the way to the ocean. Two cheerful women approach from the opposite direction, the first people I've seen in a while.

"Excuse me, is the beach very far from here?" I ask.

"Well . . ." they look at each other and their eyes widen. I don't like the look of that. The sun is setting; dusk suffuses through the forest like the color of black tea, slowly steeping in crystal clear water.

"Yeah, you can make it!" one woman says in a way that makes me think she is thankful it isn't her who still has ways to go. "Just use your spidey senses!" She gives a couple of karate chops in the air and some spidey wrist flicks like Spiderman.

I got this. "I'm on it!" I pick up my pace. Fifteen minutes later, I still can't tell how close I am. *Damn. I can't believe I didn't make it.* It's decision time: continue on and risk coming back in the dark, or turn around now? I have to act; the forest is completely still . . . I turn around. I am back on a bridge in Fern Canyon, the lowest point of the forest, where they filmed parts of *Jurassic Park*. I come to a halt. No. I cannot turn around now, even if I am trudging through the darkness on the way back. What's the difference? I march towards the ocean. Ten minutes later, I can hear the faint and triumphant sound of crashing waves. I don't know if I could have forgiven myself if I didn't make it. I was there and nearly turned back because of a misleading fear. What was I afraid of?

AS I EXIT THE DENSE FOREST, I feel the rays of the sun once again. The beach is broad and windswept. It's not inviting, per se, but I feel a sense of accomplishment. As if perfectly on cue, the couple from the parking lot stumble out of the forest. They just sprouted from a bush like my guardian angels. While I'm haggard and have built up a worthy sweat, they look refreshed, like they've just taken a nap.

Arrows of Youth

JAMES IRVINE TRAIL LOOP; PRAIRIE CREEK STATE PARK

"Hey!" I call out. "Fancy meeting you here." I balance on a shaky plank of wood placed in a small creek for crossing. "Where'd you guys just come from?" I genuinely don't know.

"We drove! Wait, did you walk here?" I nod my head as I look down at my clothes covered in dirt and sweat. His jaw drops and his eyebrows raise. "Shit, man, that's impressive. Good for you!"

"Haha, thanks, I had an existential crisis and almost turned back, but I made it. I have to get back in there to make it to the parking lot before midnight!" I enter the forest and begin my five-mile trek back through the land of *Jurassic Park*. The forest is dark and utterly quiet. I'm not afraid—quite the opposite. I sink into the sound of silence and listen to the layers of the night. The sky above the trees is a fleeting blue. I can't see further than a few feet in front of me through a thick veil of mist. The sounds of moving water echo through the trees, a trickle, a rushing, a soft falling. I stop on a bridge and breathe deep.

I see a figure. It's moving and turning up ahead of me. I slow down so I don't approach at a strange distance. But is it weirder to not come close and just say hello? Probably, so why don't I just do it? I keep my distance for the entire way back, yet the light I'm using to see almost reaches her. I can barely perceive her long hair, but I think it's a woman.

"Thanks for sharing your light!" she calls back to me on the home stretch.

"Oh, hey there!" I call back. I make my way up to her to say hello. *Should have done this a long time ago.*

"The forest at night is so peaceful," I tell her. "It's wild to think that it was just me and you in there, amongst all of this."

"Yeah, I'm glad you came along with a light," she says as she fumbles with something in her hands. "I didn't bring my phone. Sometimes we need to just disconnect." She shows me the object she's holding, a multi-colored tree root. She's right. I've been alternating between listening to books and music while hiking, but I decide to start leaving my phone.

"It looks like a clam!" I say. *That was a strange thing to say.* She laughs. It feels like we know each other without having to say much.

"I'm going to put it in my garden. I think it's beautiful." She studies the iridescent root.

"It is," I truthfully reply. I still can't make out the features of her face in the dark. "Have a great night; I hope the root finds a lovely place in your garden." We say goodbye as if we're going in separate directions, but continue to walk next to each other. Our cars are the last ones in the foggy parking lot, lit by the lustrous moon. I see the black outline of the mountain on the other side of the prairie. I get in my car and turn on the engine. The headlights beam through the night sky.

There aren't any bustling restaurants in Trinidad for dinner, especially during Covid-19. I go to Murphy's, the cheerful market that has become somewhat of a home base. I pick up barbecue chicken and broccoli salad and drive down to the beach, not knowing where to go to eat. I find a dirt path where I hear the crashing waves and pull my car into the lookout over the beach to eat under the stars.

Back at the house, I enter my room through the side door. After I've settled in I hear clicking, then clapping, then a soft voice orchestrating dance moves. I get a message on my phone.

Hope you don't mind, I'm part of a Monday night dance class that had to be moved online during the pandemic. It'll only be an hour.

I love it! I respond. Within an hour, I fall asleep for my last night in the Redwood Forest.

FERN CANYON

Colors

Burnt orange, vanilla white, dark deep reds
Which fade.
Yellows vibrant from their surrounding
Green leaves.
The orange, where does this come from?
An evanescent sunset burns,
Becoming vivid until darkness,
The melting point, how far can it go
Without breaking,
The glory which we seek.

13

WITHOUT ASKING WHY

HERE'S A FRENCH PRESS, SOME GROUND BEANS, and a kettle sitting on a small table outside of my bedroom. I don't want to wake up the house; we're family now! I leave and go to Murphy's, the grocery store where I got dinner last night. I survey every aisle, check the deli where I got dinner, and peer left and right, but there's no hot coffee. Then, with a cold brew in my hand about to accept defeat, it hits me. A trio of roasts by the front door. I pour my cup o' joe and step into the morning sun. As I sip my coffee, I scout the online lists of hikes through ancient Redwood trees. I know I can't go wrong, so I pick one that sounds unique: the Damnation Trail. With my paper cup in hand, I approach my car in the Murphy's parking lot and notice how filthy it looks. I open the door and am hit by the putrid smell of mud.

My car's packed to the brim. When amid my normal routine back home, I declutter whenever I can. Still, I can get dirty. In fact, I often

Arrows of Youth

embrace it. I take a long whiff of the muddy interior and smile. Morgan once told me a story of being a kid in Germany with his family from the old country. He and his family entered his grandfather's Mercedes, Germany's unofficial, ubiquitous car. They were hiking through the woods so their boots were covered in mud. Morgan asked his grandfather if they should take their shoes off before getting in the car. I imagine a heartfelt moment between a man who'd experienced life and a kid eager to please.

His grandfather replied: *"The car is for us, we are not for the car."* This line has served me well when I feel I'm caring too much about my things. Our phones, our cars, our clothes—they are *things*. They are for us; we are not for them. Cars are supposed to get dirty. Wear your clothes and wear them out. Don't treat your phone as more than a thing. Morgan's inherited wisdom makes me think of the power we possess— with every seed of joy, knowledge, or expertise we plant, another soul of posterity may prosper. We'll never even know.

I keep my car clean when I can, yet a car is a means to travel. A car is a means to explore. A car is a means to enjoy life. If my car has mud splattered across the windshield and sodden leaves implanted into the floor-mats, then I know I'm living my best life. My car is part of this experience, and I want to treat it with respect. That means turning the wheels and riding along the sea or through the trees for as long as I can. A car, like a human being, wants to see the world.

THE MORNING is full of promise. I turn up the music and start to freestyle, something I've been doing to get my creative thoughts flowing. It's like poetry in motion with nobody to impress. I scream and I shout and my heart fills and fills. Tears come to my eyes; I don't think about what I'm saying, I just say the words that shine from within. I tell myself I'm doing the right thing, that I'm living my life and nobody else's. Right now, I sincerely feel it. On the 101, there's a stretch for about a quarter of a mile where the river meets the sea. A layer of fog envelopes the lagoon and the mountains that recede into the coast. Two kayakers paddle languidly from one side to the other of the sheet glass water.

In this moment, I feel more like myself than I ever have. Shouldn't that be all of life, not faking or having to do anything else but give your heart and soul to what you love? This is what I love. I could travel the world and write. I could take photographs of nature and study the connections between all things. I can be a voice of change. All I have to do is continue. In this moment, there is no past; there is no future; there's only what is—immersion in my sense of self.

I see a sign as I pass the Damnation Trail: CLOSED. *Perfect.* I keep driving without stopping and then pull over to look up other trails. There's one called the Boy Scout Tree Trail further north. It's nestled into the hills away from the beach; before I know it I'm riding along rough dirt roads with looming Redwoods overhead. It's silent and cold deep in the forest where the light barely reaches. A metallic light navigates its way through the dense forest and illuminates the uneven road. The trail is long and my body is sore from the past few days, so I decide to take it slow. After about three miles, I reach a waterfall at the bottom

of the trail; it descends the slick rock face into a small pool. There's one tree in this small meadow of dark green flora next to the pool of water. I sit on a log under the tree and pull out my journal to write. A woman approaches from the path above and catches me staring at the waterfall, waiting for it to open and reveal some hidden elven city.

"Do you know if this is the end?" Her question snaps me back into reality and I laugh after being lost in thought.

"That's what I was wondering," I reply as if we're already friends. "I think this is it, but if you want to climb over the top of the waterfall it may go further." To the side of the falls are treacherous steps, muddy from the water's spray.

"I'm going to pass, but thanks. I'm Claire." She tells me she's from Dallas and quit her job during the pandemic. It made little sense for her anymore. I feel the same way. Now we both seek answers to our questions, or maybe it isn't answers that we seek. Perhaps we just want to find somewhere that'll take us in without asking why.

"I don't know what next steps I'll take," she tells me, but she doesn't sound anxious or unsure about it. It sounds like this is the surest she's ever been in her life about anything. Her demeanor is calm, like she wouldn't be the first person to start trouble, but she'd hold her own in most situations. She quit her job and went straight to the Redwoods; that's a move I respect.

"I don't know what I'm going to do either," I say with sincerity. There's something that's brought us both out here when we didn't know where else to go. She's older than me, perhaps in the next phase of life where it isn't just about *me* anymore. Life becomes the pursuit of starting a family. Or does it? That's what we're led to believe. In Claire, I see an adventurous spirit and it brings me a sense of familiarity watching her move about this muddy plot of land. There's something whole about her. She fosters a certain grace and openness to new experiences that I appreciate.

There must be something in the calming voice of the natural world that says, *You don't need to know.* Nature brings us to the present moment. I don't think about work. I don't think about anything. I stop what I'm doing and listen to Claire speak. She tells me about the forests of Colorado. I sense experiences like these are important to her, just as they are to me. She enters my life as a soul on a similar track, but I know nothing about her. *Not really, anyway.* But I know we share a common love for the unknown. Life exists in the unknown. Life is created in the unknown. Claire smiles as we finish talking and turns back and goes up the trail. I stay back in the unknown for a while until the sun drops below the trees and the forest becomes cloaked in a shadow.

I DRIVE THROUGH CRESCENT CITY, the northernmost city in California. I can't find a store that looks like it's open. Grungy, graffiti-covered warehouses line every street with disregarded junk piled in front. The city is decrepit and depressing to drive through. I pull over for a moment to take a breath and look at the ocean before the hour-long drive back to Trinidad. As I watch a few seagulls nipping at something and then each other, I hear a tap on my window. A girl is staring at me through the glass. She looks like she's about fifteen or sixteen. She's smiling eerily, but she seems harmless. I roll the window down. There's a group of younger kids with her.

"Hello?"

"Hey, you got any alcohol?"

I guess I look trustworthy. But I'm not at a point where I'm giving alcohol to kids, even though that was me once. For my friends and me to get our hands on alcohol in high school meant we'd achieved a significant victory. But it still felt harmless. This feels different, maybe because now I'm the one who is supposed to have matured.

"No, I'm sorry," I reply.

"Any cigarettes, nicotine, weed?" she asks again, hoping for anything to shake up reality. This is what it's like to be young in a forgotten city.

"Ah, no. I'm sorry."

"You don't do any of that?" she asked in a shocked tone that seems to ask, *Have you never been young and not known where to go?*

"I don't, I'm sorry." Nope, I'm a saint. I wish I could help in some other way. I don't know what to do. They leave and continue walking along the ocean. They're all kids, like me. Kids lost in themselves. I'm digging deep to uncover who I am. They are looking to numb who they are, or maybe to have fun, find an edge, a purpose. It's an off-putting conclusion to my time in Northern California that has me thinking deeply for the rest of the drive back to Trinidad.

Whenever the thoughts of self-doubt attempt to lure me off my path, I listen to the song *Do Not Let Your Spirit Wane,* by Gang of Youths.[33] It's more than just the words. The words are backed by heart, by sound, and by a repeated, beating drum. I hope those kids find their way. Perhaps they, too, need a place that'll take them in, without asking why. I'm just trying to find my own.

Arrows of Youth

BOY SCOUT TREE TRAIL

PART TWO
HE PACIFIC NORTHWEST

A Winter's Note

This too shall pass,
A moment to ponder,
Though what lies ahead,
Is it better there, yonder?
As the leaves fall away
We'll start all anew,
Then, maybe, you'll be
The best version of you.

Time will test, it will try,
It will reason to know,
For what is time, truly,
But a reason to grow?
As I look to the sky,
There glistens a sliver,
What is beautiful now,

Continues to wither.
This moment,
It fleets.

And this moment too,
What will soon turn to joy
The dark green tree, evergreen,
Forever-green,
It is not.
A memory I've always got.

Take these with you, these
Moveable Feasts,
Make life simple,
Reflect
On moments like these.

14

COLLEGE TOWNS & STRIKING SKIES

NOW MY CAR OFFICIALLY NEEDS A RESET. The scent of mud felt manageable before; but now the smell, as Ron Burgundy succinctly put it, *stings the nostrils.* Layers of dirt from hiking through the damp forests cake the interior. It would make for an intolerable seven-hour drive to Portland. I say goodbye to my home in the Redwoods and head south for fifteen minutes to the nearest car wash. It's a slight detour, but it has to be done.

On the way I return to my Trinidad watering hole, Murphy's, for a coffee, an air freshener, and a bottle of wine. I can't show up at my buddy Ron's house in Portland empty-handed. I haven't seen Ron in four years, since our college graduation trip to Greece. That trip was the first and only time we met. It was five of us: Chris, Ron, Stew, Greg, and me, a mishmash of buddies thrown together for one half-baked adventure of island-hopping through the Greek Islands. You get to know each other after spending three weeks together sipping ouzo, crashing rental cars, and eating enough souvlaki to put on what we called the *souvlaki pouch*. After the first unforgettable night on Samos, the island where Chris's grandpa grew up, we became the Souvlaki Boys, codename for best friends. Ouzo, the milky white liquor of Greece, flowed as freely as the metaphorical river famously quoted by the Greek philosopher Heraclitus, who lived in the sixth century BC: *You never step in the same river twice*, he said. Meaning: *No two moments are the same.*[34]

The trip was a toast to new beginnings and lifelong friendships. I can't wait to see Ron after a few years of navigating "the real world." With a valuable coffee buzz and a car that smells like fresh strawberry surf wax, I leave the woods and begin the coastal ascent to California's northern neighbor, Oregon. After about an hour and a half, the highway runs parallel to a slow-moving river. I feel like a frontiersman heading into the dense Northwest, following the river to the ocean. The temperature outside drops to 37° as I roll down the windows to take in the fresh, delicious air. The smell of the trees mixing with the strawberry surf wax car freshener gives me a jolt of life every fifteen minutes when I need a slap in the face.

I can't get enough of the wonderful scent. The forest air is remarkable; it may be the ultimate cure for what ails us in this anxiety-inducing time. My senses enhance as I pass the *Welcome to Oregon* sign. Thank you, Oregon. I'm happy to be here.

THE OREGON LANDSCAPE has an unmistakable character. I immediately sense the change; the beauty is striking. The crimson sky slowly transitions into a deep purple above the teeming green fields that surround the highway in every direction. A dense layer of fog hovers in the air like a blanket and infuses the passing ghostly white trees. An intermittent rain falls upon my windshield. I pass truck after truck hauling massive logs stacked upon each other in gigantic beds. I'm officially in the Pacific Northwest.

I stop in Eugene, the home of the University of Oregon, for a pick-me-up. The sun fights to break through the fog and the town takes on the golden patina of dusk. The collegiate vibe is palpable; students wander the streets with the panache of youth; U of O sweatshirts hang in the windows of countless shops like Christmas stockings. I park close to a Starbucks for a green tea and stretch on the side of the road.

My dad, Duke, and I visited the University of Oregon on a dark spring day when I was applying for colleges. My dad thought I would love it here because of its steady rain. I would have. Quaint college towns will always hold a place in my heart, with their hearty food, fun bars, and boisterous camaraderie (when it doesn't get tribal).

To have one's memories intertwine with a place is an extraordinary wonder. I cherish the memories of being with my dad and my brother looking at colleges—what a concept! We were deciding where I'd have the most fun for the next four years. These decisions felt like the most important ones I'd ever make. Now, college is nothing but a memory. I could have been anywhere, but I wonder if my life would have been so different if I was here instead of on the California coast for those instrumental years. Would I feel the need to come here now, or would I tire of the rain? Would I feel a calling to the Pacific Northwest? Would I —the question I contemplate more than anything else—be a writer if I hadn't stuck with journalism? I pull back my hands in a stretch and turn

Arrows of Youth

my face towards the sun. There's no way to know for sure; but I did. And now, I am.

"Hello, beautiful day," I say to a passing stranger on his way out of the lot. I hold my stretch, smiling, willfully oblivious to how strange it might look. It's an emotional moment as the memories of being here as an eager college-student-to-be flood my mind. The man laughs like he's surprised by my joy. I laugh, too.

IT'S DARK WHEN I ARRIVE in Portland. The dynamic energy of the city turns my senses on high alert. There are few things I love more than arriving in a new city for the first time. A year ago, my best friends and I walked deliriously through the rainy, neon streets of Tokyo after our fourteen-hour flight. The ground glistened and reflected the skyscrapers above. I could hardly speak as my face froze in a dazzled grin. Several months later, I arrived in Dublin to meet my dad in the middle of a hailstorm. I mistakenly passed my exit and rode for about an hour along the frothy, Guinness-colored river and into the heart of the city, watching beads of ice drip down the bus window. I think of the unmistakable delight of walking at night along the Seine River in Paris, and the sounds of clinking bikes echo in my head. Those are memories, stowed arrows; I'm here to craft a new one.

I take in the reflection of the green, red, and purple lights radiating from the Willamette River on the way to Ron's apartment. Boats sail past and gleam in the darkness. Something's clearly unusual. Restaurants are closed and there aren't many people out wandering the streets. I'm in the heart of where much of the rioting following George Floyd's death took place over the summer; I can't overlook the obvious impact that lingers in the air. The world needs healing, and I hope to be a part of that process. I'm glad I'm here during this unique time, if only to make a stranger laugh. When the world opens up, we will once again celebrate. But now is a chance to be the light that the world needs. Travel is no less beautiful in this solemn season; I feel my purpose is to be living proof.

"Vince!" I hear my name as I drag the bags from my car. I spin around to see Ron's smiling face.

"Hey, Ronald! What's happening, buddy?"

It's so good to see Ron. We catch up on the walk to his apartment. He tells me about dental school; I tell him about the trip. We settle into his comfortable two-person apartment a block from the river, where I'm greeted by his amiable hound, Lola. For dinner, Ron takes me to a Vietnamese spot with an outdoor seating area. It's empty on this frigid Oregon night. Still, we share a couple of frosty beers and steaming bowls of pho full of tripe, beef, and vegetables. We discuss life and this peculiar situation over the heady soup. Back at Ron's, the laughter continues over a couple of glasses of whisky until Ron passes out on the couch with his glass in his hand.

Just like old times, buddy.

RON'S ASSEMBLAGE OF NATIONAL PARKS

Caught in Webs So Finely Spun

Inspired by Walt Whitman's A Noiseless Patient Spider [35]

A spider clings to web it flings,
Launching forth its filament;
A spider thus suspends from air,
Isolated, twirling, its fabric ductile as wire,
Sustains its weight,
Its patient gait,
Within it has all that it needs.

And you, O soul, you search for life to hold onto,
Caught in webs so finely spun,
For place that makes you feel like you,
O soul, break from this mesh to spin your own
So that when you're old and grown,
You'll have a web, beautiful art,
You have a life to live, so start.

15

BREAKING THROUGH IN PORTLAND

LOLA GREETS ME IN THE MORNING with tender eyes. The lights of the neighborhood high-rise apartments gently turn on as the sky turns from a deep blue into a subdued pink dawn. Christmas trees that have been on all night glow in the apartments across the way and add a multicolored radiance to the morning. The city wakes as I do—with the rising sun. Ron leaves for dental school after we share coffee in the living room. It's just Lola and me. I feel like part of the family.

I have the day to explore Portland, which means getting from here to the other side of the city. It's a journey of discovery to travel by foot, as I never know what I'll pass or what might capture my attention. Through traveling, we expose ourselves to alternative ways of living as the unfamiliar seizes our senses and makes us come alive. The key to growth is exposing ourselves as often as possible to new situations, new people, and novel ideas that we aren't comfortable with. According to

Arrows of Youth

Jordan Peterson in *12 Rules for Life*:

> *So much of what you could be will never be forced by necessity to come forward. This is a biological truth, as well as a conceptual truth. When you explore boldly, when you voluntarily confront the unknown, you gather information and build your renewed self out of that information.*

To voluntarily confront the unknown is to step into chaos, where we're required to think differently and challenge our preconceptions of who we are. We improve our street smarts, build our character, and strengthen our sense of self. We aren't finite. This can be the most exciting aspect of being human. According to Peterson, this is the path to realizing our most capable self. He writes:

> *Researchers have recently discovered that new genes in the central nervous system turn themselves on when an organism is placed in a new situation. These genes code for new proteins. These proteins are the building blocks for new structures in the brain. This means that a lot of you is still nascent, in the most physical of senses, and will not be called forth by stasis. You have to say something, go somewhere, and do things to get turned on. And, if not . . . you remain incomplete, and life is too hard for anyone incomplete.*

There is no perfect self, yet by exposing ourselves to new experiences—there's always room for growth. I lay on the floor and go through a quick workout with my portable bands while listening to *The Model Health Show with Shawn Stevenson.*[36] Stevenson has the self-proclaimed 9 to 5 Millionaire Jemal King on the show. Their conversation is positive fuel for my mind and lights a fire in my belly, creating an intoxicating combination. Jemal King is the 9 to 5 Millionaire because he urges people to pursue what's in their hearts while still holding down a 9 to 5 job. In a passionate tone, as if he's on stage in front of a crowd of five thousand, King says:

> *People in their 9 to 5 get depressed, they're wondering how come life is not how they planned it. It's because they made their vehicle their destination, and their destination their vehicle.*

We can break down our goals, dreams, and aspirations into means goals versus destination goals. Happiness is a destination. Love is a destination. Freedom is a destination. Once you're there, nothing can surpass that human emotion. Destination goals are our reason for being. A 9 to 5 is a vehicle because it's a means to get to the destination. King knows this story well, as he comes from a family of Chicago police officers who turned their jobs into their destinations. King put everything he had into sports as a young man, but when he lost the ability to continue, he felt lost. Sports were his identity, and he didn't know what next steps to take.

He became a cop like the other men in his family, but he knew he had a great deal more to give. When other officers ate doughnuts and watched the same movie over and over in their car, King used his off-time to work out, educate himself, and most importantly, drive around looking at decrepit areas of Chicago to invest in. He became the richest cop in Chicago through real estate investing without leaving his 9 to 5. Anything is possible when we believe in ourselves.

The world will tell us when to settle, but only *we* decide when to succumb to the pressure or turn up the heat. Rain clouds turn the early morning sky into a wash of grey and white—perfect exploring weather. After a shower, I hit the streets on foot, eager to get lost in the Portland rain. I walk along the river and stop to look back at the city's iconic bridges. I walk through the grass where the summer's biggest protests took place and wonder about it all. Dense evergreen hills surround Portland in every direction.

Sprinkled in the sea of green like dustings of dark, chalky clay are colors evoking the onset of winter. Crunchy amber autumn leaves fall from the changing trees and sweep through the city streets in gusts. I ponder how the city must have changed through the ages, yet still preserves its wonderfully distinct character. Portland's identity comprises burnished copper buildings reminiscent of old timber mills, the natural surroundings of the changing season, and the modern, slate blue downtown sky-rises. It all glistens and comes alive in the rain. This is its essence.

THE THOUGHTS CONTINUE as I listen to Jemal King: *What are you doing with your life? Shouldn't you be working like everybody else?* This voice is what Steven Pressfield refers to as "the Resistance" in his influential book, *The War of Art*,[37] coming to drag me into the pit with the snakes. *This is a sign.* As I gaze acutely into the lapping waves of the opaque Willamette River, I question what I'm truly afraid of. My reflection stares back; I look into my soul. And then it hits me—one of the most powerful lessons from *The War of Art*:

> *Resistance feeds on fear. We experience resistance as fear, but fear of what? Fear of being ridiculous. Fear of launching into the void, of hurtling too far out there, fear of passing some point of no return, beyond which we cannot recant, cannot reverse, cannot rescind, but must live with this cocked up choice for the rest of our lives. These aren't the real fear, the Master fear. Fear that we will succeed. That we can access the powers we secretly know we possess. That we can become the person we sense in our hearts we truly are.*

This is why I'm here, a solitary being beneath the saturnine Oregon sky. I crave to know the story of the world, of the people that I meet, of the great cities and the cold, natural landscapes; it's my dream to make the world my home. We must dream so absurdly big that people won't understand. That's how it should be—the world makes little sense, so why should we? People only have what they know: work during the week so you can escape on the weekends. But I'm not willing to settle for that.

I know there's more to life, a harmonious existence to tap into. If I can feel this much love for the people I meet, if I can feel the fire burning within me that only needs to be stoked, if I can sense the magic bursting from every second and every breath, then there must be something worth striving for that transcends what we call our daily routine. As long as I'm alive, *I want to live.* And when the time comes to leave this Earth, I want to know without a shadow of a doubt that I gave it everything I had. There won't be anything left to take, not a regret, nor an *I love you* unsaid. The world doesn't need more people fitting into the mold. Civil rights leader and author Howard Thurman once said:

> *Don't ask what the world needs. Ask what makes you come alive, and go do it. Because what the world needs is people who have come alive.*

WITH MY CAMERA IN HAND, I walk past two men spray painting a vibrant mural on the outskirts of downtown. The art adds a burst of playful charm to the dreary grey street. It's something to make you stop, pause, and wonder, like a lost red balloon amid a stormy sky. I find my way into Powell's Bookstore, one of the legendary independent bookstores of the United States. To my delight, there are others perusing the aisles, spending time amongst the endless rows of stories.

I scan the bookmarks at the front of the store and pick up a blue wooden one with an owl. I don't know which labyrinthian aisle to head down, so I randomly cut into one and as if by fate come across a section on the nineteenth-century American poet Walt Whitman. Whitman captures the essence of 1800s America, the spirit of a new nation finding its footing. I pull out his essential body of poetry, *Leaves of Grass*,[38] from the row of texts I suspect rarely see the light of day.

Brilliance laying dormant, waiting for the curious eye of a wandering soul. I read the poem *Song of Myself*:

> *I celebrate myself, and sing myself,*
> *And what I assume you shall assume,*
> *For every atom belonging to me as good belongs to you.*

Whitman's poem provides a glimpse not only into an erstwhile age, but the soul of a man. A man like me. Reading, photography, poetry, any sort of art creates an invisible web through time and space that unite our spirits as human beings. Whitman lived during the Civil War and captured the essence of an expanding, tumultuous nation. I live in the 21st century and strive to impart my love for what it means to be alive in this day and age. Both Whitman and I write to better know ourselves.

A book catches my eye amongst the dusty titles: *The Better Angel.*[39] During the Civil War, Whitman became an angel to the fallen soldiers that filled the hospitals to the brim. He found meaning by caring for these soldiers who had nothing left to live for. All they wanted from him was a piece of licorice or something to ease the pain in their throats. All they wanted was for somebody to care for them and prove they weren't just another hospital bed, but a soul worth noticing. History makes me infinitely grateful. I buy *The Better Angel,* and *On the Road* by Jack Kerouac.[40]

IT RAINS ALL MORNING as I head to the quintessential northeast part of Portland known for its eclectic streets. I walk around Mississippi Street and the Alberta Arts District, although with nothing open all I can really do is take in the street art. That's fine with me. I buy an espresso and a salted chocolate chip cookie and sit at the restaurant's outdoor patio.

I pull out *On the Road* while I wait for the rain to let up. It pours down hard on the steel roof overhead. I can't think of anything I'd rather be doing. I read and dip the cookie into the coffee. I watch it fall apart and drift to the edges of the cup like Pangea. Kerouac searches for what lights him up in America's great cities: New York, Denver, San Francisco, Los Angeles, and New Orleans—he hitchhikes with farmers and knocks around with his buddy Dean. He doesn't know how to find joy in life, and he tries to fill a void through escaping. It was the fifties, the age of consumerism. Are we any better today?

The rain stops and a golden afternoon light glistens atop the city streets. The fresh scents of the natural environment pervade the city after the long rain; I can't stop smiling. The smells of wet pavement, rich coffee, and vibrant flowers waft through the streets. The early afternoon air is brilliant and revitalizing. I grab one of the orange electric bikes found around the city and weave my way through all of Portland, crossing bridge after bridge over trains and rivers. I feel utterly free, having not ridden a bike in ages.

I head for the Northwest part of town to explore Forest Park before sunset. People run through the last of the autumn leaves and I can see my breath outlined before me as I trudge through the peripheral neighborhoods. I spend time lost in the park as I make my way to Witch's Castle. It's an unusual structure that stands out amongst the mossy forest because of the striking purple spray paint covering the crumbling stones. I don't know why it's here, but it gives people like me something to explore. The sun goes down as I exit the forest. I call Ron.

"Hey Ron, can you come pick me up? My phone's about to die and I can't get this bike to work again." I'm not exactly sure where I am, and make the call to play it safe rather than trying to figure out how to get back on my own.

"You're so cute!" I spin around without thinking as two laughing girls walk by; I'm caught like a deer in the headlights.

"Thanks, so are you!" The response comes without my doing. We lock eyes, but everything is fuzzy after my third espresso of the day and the light emanating from the sign I stand beside. The girl has long curly hair and a fleece zipped up to her chin. I smile and try to put the pieces together. Before I know it she's several streets away, and I'm left with my thoughts and a dazzled expression. Why is it so gut-wrenching to say what's on our mind without thinking? Four words, a compliment, a laugh, and a joke. She spoke up and made me feel something real. She made me believe that I'm a soul worth noticing.

We are all worth noticing. When we're noticed, we become confident in who we are. When we're confident with who we are, we're able to give back to another soul who needs love, too. My heart is full of love; I'm floating and okay with it.

"Vince!" Ron pulls up in his Subaru. I run across the street and get into the car.

"Thanks, buddy!" Ron, Lola and I take a walk along the river to bring the day to a close. The neon lights from the boats reflect on the smooth black water like an impressionist oil painting. As the city turns in, we gaze into the lights on the water and the sky devoid of stars. Still,

I know they're there, waiting to ignite—the dormant potential of a star-less night. After dinner, Ron gives me a Superman sticker from work; I put it into my journal. It reads *Great Patient!* It's a sticker you'd give to a kid after pulling a tooth. It's the best souvenir I could have asked for. The stop was brief, but when I return we'll celebrate, for Portland has captured my heart.

Mask

Still trying to smile,
Underneath this mask of cloth,
Covering my face.

16

A ROSE WITH PETALS & THORNS

S T. JOHN'S BRIDGE IS A FADED LIGHT BLUE set against the backdrop of Portland's abundant green hills. Ron tells me to stop here to check out Cathedral Park on my way out. When a local tells you to check out a spot, don't let them down. It will be worth it. As has been customary, I cross several other bridges to get to Cathedral Park, traveling back and forth over the water like a skipping rock.

My family group chat is blowing up my phone. The family group chat is a recent phenomenon. It isn't just one or two close family members—it's about twenty of us. I smile at the pictures and the memories of my grandfather Dicky that pour in from my relatives. It's December 9th, my grandpa's birthday. There was nobody like Dicky; he called me Lefty. Dicky loved all people and only wanted to make them laugh. I think about him even in the last phase of his life when it was clear how badly he was suffering from diabetes. Yet he continued fighting to maintain his infectious, merry spirit.

"Ah, this hat makes me look silly!" he would say, referring to the cap he had to wear to protect his scalp. He never cursed, but he loved to act goofy. As I walk along the outskirts of Cathedral Park, I think about the days I spent with him. My grandfather went to the racetrack every day when he wasn't working. Santa Anita or Hollywood Park were the favorites—if one was closed, he'd be at the other. His friends and his community were there; going to the racetrack brought him genuine joy. I remember pulling up to my grandparent's house as a kid around eleven or twelve. I wore an oversized blazer, and long black hair would hang in front of my face as I rubbed my eyes from sleeping on the drive over.

Orange persimmons dangled low from the trees that led to the front door of the San Fernando Valley cottage. I'd maneuver around the crushed fruit on the ground—a hop from one stone to the next, then a duck under the tree. The driveway smelled of freshly cut green grass that baked in the sun, day after day. The feeling of stepping from the car into the gravel driveway contains the memory, like a note in a glass bottle.

Red, pink, and white rose bushes covered the front windows of the house. The air was dry and would sap my energy as if I was walking through the desert. My grandparents were young and full of life before I felt like I came into my own. That's the relationship between grandparents and grandkids. There will always be that void of understanding, but that's the magic that can make the relationship special. Grandparents and grandkids understand each other differently than parents and kids. There's a camaraderie, a love between opposite souls that represents the bookends of life. Between them lays what I find myself in now, the row of books between the bookends, not the beginning and not the waning dusk, but the heat of noon when we spend our days trying to understand.

I now remember Dicky as somebody different from the man I knew. I hear stories of him in his prime, as strong as an ox and full of indefatigable energy. It was challenging to see that energy decline, especially for my dad, Vincent, and my uncles, Jimmy and Nels. These are his three sons. They embody his spirit, just as I strive to do. Such is the way of life. From a child, to a man, to a grandfather, then back into the earth to take on the life of a rose, or perhaps as my grandpa would have liked it, the dirt beneath a horse's hooves at the starting gate of Santa Anita.

WHEN WE'D ARRIVE at the house, Dicky was already at the track; he wouldn't miss a race if he could help it. Dicky and one of his best friends, the hilarious Mel Brooks, socialized like kids on their lunch break. They'd laugh and tell stories, drink coffee and Coca-Cola, and diligently read the racing form. The soda wasn't healthy, nor the gambling, but it kept their spirits young. This was where they felt the happiest. My grandfather never drank alcohol, but he always had a cold Coke in a glass with ice sitting on the white tablecloth, as sugar was his only drug of choice. The drink looked incredible on a hot day.

Hovering around the table or sitting at one adjacent would surely be one or two fellas who looked like they were in the mafia. One in particular always wore a suit and a turtleneck sweater straight out of *Goodfellas*. My uncle Casey drove with Dicky every day. Casey would stolidly read the racing form and sip a cup of black coffee. When he saw my dad, my brother, and me approach their table at the Turf Club, he would shine a comforting smile. His eyes, too, would smile as his face softened.

We'd pull up chairs and sit at the surrounding tables. My grandfather was the sun; we revolved around him like planets and craved his warmth. Everybody did. He would tell my brother and me we could be jockeys, although it was a shame; we weren't small enough. My grandpa respected jockeys more than anyone—the names are tough to forget: *Corey Nakatani, Mike Smith, Laffit Pincay Jr.*

Jockeys are tough as nails. Although, as we'd watch them click and clack through the tunnel out to the starting gate, they gave off the friendliest energy which enraptured my grandpa for his entire life. I would try to read the form, but my eyes would glaze over the esoteric stats, which Hemingway called "*The true art of fiction.*"[41] An art, indeed. The racing form lays out the characteristics of the race down to the trivial: the horse's age, fitness, and weight; their trainer and their history; where the horses were bred; which performed best on dry dirt, rainy slush, or turf; and recent results. Those like Dicky experienced in studying the form can create links between the different factors, like the stars of a constellation.

He had a formula. I had no idea what I was reading. Therefore, I went with whoever had the coolest name.

"*Dad,*" I'd say while giving him over my twenty bucks for the day, "*I'll take whoever you take . . . to win.*" Duke would confidently rattle off three obscure names to win, place, and show as he'd hand over his lot to my dad. To win means to come in first place, to place means coming in second, to show means coming in third. That, I knew. I don't think my brother knew how to read the form either. He just got lucky.

MY DAD, DUKE, DICKY AND ME IN A JOVIAL NUTSHELL

MY ATTEMPT AT READING THE RACING FORM; SANTA ANITA PARK

The sound of the horn would blast through the halls and through our skin. The race was about to begin . . .

"AND . . . THEY'RE OFF!" The horses left the starting gate like bullets from a gun.

"He's pacing himself, don't worry!" Dicky exclaimed. Our pick to win hung towards the back of the pack. "There's the move. He's making his move!" The vivid colors of the jockey's uniforms would blend with the track; they became one brown cloud of colorful dust as they hugged the gate around the turn, rounding the home stretch. Neck and neck until the end, when Laffit Pincay Jr. broke away and won. Ten-to-one odds. My brother won a hundred bucks. I'd never been so jealous.

I didn't appreciate the memory then, but that's being a kid; we never know the good old days are the good old days. We're often not aware at the moment, but that day, that year that flies by, that person, we will always be them. Nostalgia, like the antiquated wooden racetrack that no longer stands, is beautiful. It's a part of history, our history. We're living in the good old days. The memories we make are the memories we have forever, arrows to craft and cherish.

I WATCH THE LEAVES fall from the winter trees on the chill December morning. I think about my grandpa's smile and his warmth. He did what made him happy. He loved being alive and nothing could dim that light. When I see a subtle red rose, I think of days at the racetrack. At the onset of spring, the smell of roses drifted through the racetrack grounds when the races would begin. Dicky was human and had incredible gifts as well as faults, just as a rose is a rose with its petals and its thorns. Yet, my grandfather's legacy is a good one. He lived for others.

He lived to share his light, regardless of whether it would be reciprocated. My grandpa was a good man.

I lap the park to move my legs and then walk to the edge of the river. A few rusting boats float next to the shore as if in a slumber they'll never wake from. Their rotting wooden exteriors blend with the rippling grey water. The scene is somber, a tranquil shade of gloom that characterizes the morning. After some time, I get in my car and drive over the train tracks and into the outskirts of Portland where I pull over to get some gas. A couple of gas station attendants come over to my car to help me pump; it's an Oregon thing I'm not privy to.

"It's fine. I got it!" It seems rather unnecessary.

"We have to help you, bro," one of the large men reluctantly responds, as if he realizes it's an outdated job.

"So, this is considered the outskirts of Portland?" I say, trying to spark some conversation with the young kid pumping the gas. He's wearing a Louis Vuitton face mask and gives a hasty nod. I guess he isn't into talking. Another man jaunts over to finish pumping the gas. I see the possibility of a fresh conversation and take another stab at it.

"How are you doing, my man?"

He takes his time to respond, as if considering my motives.

"Not too bad," he says after a pause. "Just trying to get through the day. It's my birthday. I'm going to get fucked up." He's big, bigger than the other two, with a belly that hangs out of his shirt quite low, a few feet from the ground. He looks over at me and gives a childlike smile with his entire face; his eyes change, and I see the corners of his mouth rise far beyond the constraints of the mask.

Arrows of Youth

After taking off, I begin to flow down the interstate like a fish in a school until the cars come to an abrupt stop. There's something on the road in the distance—several things. I can't make out what they are. A man and woman come into view on the shoulder of the highway. The man's wearing an oversized Boston Celtics basketball jersey and black speed shades—the glasses most commonly found on the rack at the gas station that look like cheap heat vision goggles.

The couple is sprinting in my direction; they run into the street like it's a game of *Frogger*! *How does this happen?* They grab handfuls of clothes that are spewed all over the highway and when they make it back to the side of the road, the woman throws her hand into the air in a triumphant gesture. It looks part like a thank you to everybody who has stopped and part primal-queen victory *hurrah!* I can't help but break out laughing. I pass their car a quarter of a mile down the road. It's pulled-over with the lights blinking and the doors open. What has to happen for several massive piles of clothes to fly out of your car into oncoming traffic?

On one side of the highway I drive along an obsidian creek; on the other, a rusty red train the color of Mars chugs beside me as if it carries in each cart the essence of the Pacific Northwest. The colors of the train blend with the brush and the looming trees to create an identity. The embedded hints of bright oranges and yellows of the changing season and the dark wheat color of the fields make the landscape absolutely stunning.

As I enter Washington, the trees become more ghostly, almost as if frost from a prehistoric freeze clings on to their branches. Some icy trees appear purple and have a luminous aura to them. Others are a mossy bright green from the incessant rain. I drive through the backwoods of Washington atop rolling hills, passing sprawling fields and farms. Smoke rises from chimneys like vivid puffs from a pipe into the interminable rain. I roll down the window to smell the wood-burning fires that mix so wonderfully with the deep forest air. I pass brown and black cows, sheep, and horses. Back on the highway I pass countless eighteen-wheelers hauling massive lumber carts filled to the brim with the corpses of dead trees. It makes me sad after spending so much time in the forests.

Every so often I pass quirky espresso kiosks with vaulted roofs like European Christmas markets. They have actual humans working in them! *I'm going to stop at the next one I see,* I tell myself through the softly tapping rain. They're all relatively similar and cheerful with Christmas lights draped from their roofs. These are the signs of the season, and I love seeing them. I stop at a kiosk and walk through the muddy parking lot instead of driving through. I need to stretch my legs.

"I love these espresso kiosks. Very cheerful!"

"Oh, you're not from Washington then," she replies dismissively.

"I'm not, just visiting. I love it here." When I tell locals I love their home, I usually get the same response: a look that says, *Why?* I guess because your home is not like my own, because every place has an identity that I long to explore, because the rain and the mud and the deep smell of trees transport me not just to a different part of the world, but to a different time and space altogether. Because exploring makes me better understand who I am, and it's all I long to do. I wish I could tell her this, but she's busily turning from me to the cars pulling alongside the kiosk.

Arrows of Youth

"Thank you," I smile as I take the espresso from her hands in the paper cup. I sip it under the thatched roof so the rainwater won't dilute the bitter taste. *I needed this.* At about 3:30 p.m., I cruise down the highway and listen to the symphony of the rumbling car—*the cello perhaps*—with the rain pattering against the windshield—*snares, winds, horns.* I turn down the music and savor the melody of the tapping raindrops. When I reach Olympic National Park in the evening, it hits me. I've driven practically the entire Pacific Coast, from San Diego to the top of Washington.

This puts a smile on my face. I stop at Ruby Beach, a marvel of Olympic National Park, before heading into the town of Forks. It's pouring rain as I pull into the empty parking lot. I put on my rain boots and head down the swampy path to the beach. It's like nothing I've ever seen. Fallen trees cover the entire beach, like a burial ground for giants. The sky is a mixture of burning orange and fierce dark grey. I've never seen a place that's so raw. It could be the year 2020 or 100,000 BC and I don't know if there would be a difference. The rain falls, the ocean churns, and the waves crash. Here it seems they never stop beating. If they did, the planet would slip away. The trees on the beach grow and sway in the roaring winds to fall and soften from the sea. I'm stunned while watching it happen—life is taking place, unaware of my existence.

I'M DRAWN TO OBSERVE THE PATTERNS of nature because all I have to do is watch. Something extraordinary is taking place when the world churns and breathes, something archaic. We can express the action: a tree falls on the beach. Yet, it's sometimes impossible to put into words the emotion nature evokes. There's a beauty in that inability to capture the human feeling. That's the thing about art; it's the human's attempt at portraying something we all experience yet find it hard to say. Where words won't do, perhaps a color, or a line, or a photograph, or a chord, will. The viewer may interpret what's being said for themselves; a novel thought arises. Art, like nature, eclipses mere communication. It addresses the heart directly.

The waves crash, the sun sets, the rain falls, the trees sway; as I watch life unfold, I feel a change on the inside. At this moment, I'm at peace. I let go of my sense of self that worries about the trivialities of life and, in doing so, I connect with who I truly am. Then I want to write, because it makes me feel alive. I want to capture the love I feel for the world as best as I can. That's a daily endeavor I feel is worth pursuing.

I've always been one who would rather sit back and subtly observe than fight for my time to shine. I also realize how this has changed since I've gotten older, but it's happened in a way that feels natural to me and aligns with the person I've always been. I don't really care who wins the game; I just want to play. This personality trait was most apparent when I was young. As a younger brother in a big family flush with outgoing personalities, I'd find myself either hovering around my parents at family gatherings or off to the side as the festivities wore on. This brought me comfort. I've always looked up to my older cousins, my uncles and aunts, Dicky, and my strong, caring, jubilant grandmother Pat. I don't know how I got thrown into such an incredible group of people. But as I grew up and developed interests and a distinguishable personality of my own, I would still keep my thoughts to myself unless pressed. *Why is that?* I didn't feel the need to compare.

I know I want to express who I am and always have, but I never felt a genuine need. My family just wanted to learn more about me; I love them for that. Before developing opinions I care deeply about or even feeling fully like myself, not speaking up may have been construed as a sign that I had nothing worth saying. When it came time to say something, I felt the pressure that it better be worthwhile. So I kept quiet. They just wanted me to talk, to have a laugh together, to learn. Maybe I didn't see that.

Often there are no answers to why we are the way we are. I ask every day what it means to be me. I question the universe about the unexplainable circumstances of life. But we as human beings continue to persevere in our own ways, irrespective of the challenges we endure. This is what it means to be alive, for I can stand on this beach and my past doesn't matter, my circumstances don't matter, and my pain doesn't matter. All that matters is this very moment. I'm without an identity—I can be anything I long to be.

As a kid, I'd feel content off to the side watching the party, listening to the conversation, developing my thoughts and opinions, yet seldom conveying them. But I noticed the ways people interacted with one another, and I noted the joy and the excitement or the hurt, and I wondered about it. I wondered why we feel the way we do. I continue to question what goes into making us all that we are. And that's what inspires me now more than ever: our interactions and connections as human beings. Those days of being a kid and patiently observing brought me to this beach. Now, I feel that I have something worth saying.

I return to nature as my unyielding source of inspiration because there's no rhyme or reason; there's just being. Sometimes it's difficult to come to grips with the fact that this is who I am. We change every day, and when we're something we weren't before, we question who we are. People won't recognize us anymore, and that makes us afraid. We've lost our illusory grip of control. When I wonder about what it means to be a human and what role I may play in this world, I return to the sounds of the natural world. The sound of rain pounding against the shore is a sort of meditation. Nature won't ask me for anything, not to step up or be something or lead. Still, it provides an answer to a question I don't know how to ask in any other way: *What am I on this Earth to do?*

It's okay to listen if that's all I want to do. And when I'm ready to take a stand and let my spirit shine, I will. I don't know when that will be. I don't know if it's now. There's nothing to force; nobody to impress; nothing I have to be. I'm me, the same person I've always been. As life continues and I find my place in this world, that person will step up, confident and strong, when the time comes. That person will stand up with the same sincere energy as the falling rain and communicate who he is. I think we'll know when we're meant to break free. The white noise will fade away. All we'll hear is our beating heart and we'll feel nothing but love. And then we'll know we're alive in this body and this soul; we won't be in our past nor waiting for the future, and nothing will be the same. *Maybe that day is today.*

It looks like there is a lighthouse on the horizon, although it's obscured. I wander around the beach not looking for anything in particular, just heeding my curiosity. I find roses placed on a rock, a note of dark red like the ripped out heart of a fallen giant. I wonder who left them here, maybe as a symbol to remember a soul no longer with us. I think of my grandpa, Dicky. As long as we talk about our ancestors and tell their stories, their laughs travel through the generations. Their glinting smiles, passions, and subtleties, if we allow them to be, are with us always.

My grandpa is here with me, urging me to embrace life with everything I have. I strive to live in a way that will cause my grandkids to wonder and laugh as I do when I hear stories of Dicky. He did so much good with his life. He had his accomplishments and was a famous TV dad on *Eight Is Enough*. But that's not what he's remembered for. At least, that's not why I remember him. When we're nothing but dust in the wind, our accolades and our achievements won't matter. What will matter is the lives we've touched, the memories we made for others to hold on to for the time that they have. That time goes in the blink of an eye. The night falls, and I'm enveloped in loving darkness.

Soul Explorer

A cleansing walk beneath the night,
Rain which lays down on the sea,
A look out there to know I'm free.
The stars which shine, beautiful light,
No need to struggle, nor to fight
My thoughts I simply let them be
I turn within, the real me,
To understand the more I write.

The soul connects to time and space,
The pen a ship exploring deep
What seems so cloaked in mystery.
The dark, I feel its full embrace,
My body poised, ready to leap,
Gone back again through history.

17
REVELATION

FROM RUBY BEACH I MAKE MY way to Forks, Washington. As I drive into town I pass a sign overhanging the single main road that reads: *Seasons Greetings, Vampires Not Welcome!* I didn't know this is the town where the vampire movie *Twilight* was set; I can't help but laugh about that. Christmas lights hang from every building; they imbue the dark night with the fluorescent color of the season. Posted on many of the buildings are posters with #ForksStrong for the world to see. I get the impression that the pandemic has hit this town hard, like many other small towns that rely on tourism. It's a sad state of affairs we're in, yet there's an inspiring, unyielding light in Forks.

I pull over to pick up groceries at the central market and step into slushy potholes in the parking lot, filled from the persistent rain. I go with some chicken and vegetables for dinner and a few other random essentials: whisky, nuts, beef jerky. It doesn't feel like an ordinary market where you run in and grab your groceries while avoiding conversation. I overhear laughter amongst friends. I see soulful humans behind the hot food counter, patiently serving chicken drumsticks to little kids with their parents and making the kids laugh with a sly joke. There's something special here, and I don't think it's just the grocery store, but *the community* that embodies the term #ForksStrong. I try to make conversation with the clerk at the checkout line. She's a young woman, from what I can tell with our masks on.

"Hey there, do you have any recommendations for things to do around Olympic?" She doesn't respond, as her mind seems elsewhere. Maybe she's tired, or she's hurt, I can't be sure. I don't know what this job means to her or how she's been handling the pandemic; I don't know her name or her story, and all I want to do is make her smile.

"Oh, sorry," she shakes her head as if awakening from a daydream. "No, not really."

She's distracted. A strange pause hangs in the air between us, the few seconds that separate pain and love, a void unfilled by the single question that I can't seem to ask: *Are you okay?*

"We live here and we have seen a little of the park," remarks the kind woman standing in line a few feet behind me. Her hair is slightly damp and unkempt, but she's kind; I can tell from the sleepy eyes that hide behind her reading glasses. At the moment, I feel like I need glasses. Everything becomes vague as my face flushes, like there's a spotlight shining on me. I can tell the woman's forcing a subtle smile, as if she senses what I'm trying to do with my innocuous questioning. I smile at her as if we're on the same team. *We all are, and I just want them to feel it.*

"We forget that we're rich," she says as she shrugs her shoulders. I'm overcome with gratitude by the powerful sentiment. My questions found an answer. The things we have don't make us rich; I think we've learned this during the pandemic. I thought this town was on its last leg—I should have paid more attention to the sign on the market: #Forks-Strong. The people of Forks are rich in connection, for they are clearly there for one another. The people in the grocery store are part of the community—I can sense this when I overhear their interactions. They know one another and they support each other's businesses. The people of Forks are rich in heart. They hang their Christmas lights despite the pouring rain. It just makes the lights shine brighter.

THIS PANDEMIC WON'T BEAT US because as human beings, we will always fight to find a semblance of joy no matter what we must endure. I feel called to the Pacific Northwest to create a life I love. I'm on this adventure to show the world, and myself, how good people really are when we do whatever it takes to be there for each other. This isn't a trip to forget about the world. It's one to better understand it. Challenges will always find their way to make us stumble; yet without the difficulties, we'd never know what's possible to overcome. I intend to be a light in this world, a bridge between people. But today, when I needed an answer, I found a guiding light in another human being.

I pull around the gravel driveway where there are two buildings side by side. One is the owner's house, the other is a work garage beneath the room I'm staying in. As I fiddle with the keys, trying to open the door next to the garage, a voice comes from the house.

Arrows of Youth

"Hey there; other door, around the side!" A man and a woman come out of the house and into the rain. A dog runs through the front door into the dark driveway.

"Ah, right, thank you!" I rush around the corner to get under cover. "Have a great night!" They smile as they get in their car. The dog shares a few barks from the door. I stumble in the front door and head up the stairs. The first thing I do when I get inside is open the windows to listen to the rain. I make dinner, and as soon as the scent of it fills the small apartment, it begins to feel like home.

I don't remember a particular time when a flip switched and I became interested in cooking; all I know is I was a kid who loved to eat. How food differs from culture to culture, region to region, fascinated me as a kid, and does even more now. My stepmom Eileen taught me how to cook. In my house growing up, the kitchen was the place to lean against the counter, laugh, and experience each other's company around mealtimes. My dad was the one who always had withered grapes, apples, and fruit of all kinds out on the kitchen counter. For the most part, Eileen did the cooking. She passed down the kitchen subtleties that inspired a lifelong love of feeding my body and soul through my own ability.

I cut up the brussel sprouts and turn on my music. I place the sprouts in the cast-iron skillet face down with olive oil and cover them to simmer. A recipe can only teach you so much. The nuances that turn an ordinary dish into the extraordinary come from either trial and error, or the guidance of a kitchen sage, one like Eileen. These nuances may include how long to heat a pan and how to tell if it's hot before laying down a steak; how freshly chopped herbs can transform a meal; and of course, the importance of cooking pasta *al dente*. These things come with practice. This has been one of the underlying blessings of the pandemic—we're cooking at home. Those averse to cooking before have hopefully learned a thing or two.

When we share what we love with others, such as kitchen skills, we're planting seeds of joy. It's part of the gift of being alive to make somebody *feel* something, be it through the delicious taste of the food we share, or by passing down the expertise honed from years in the kitchen. This transfer of kitchen prowess does more than give another human being practical life skills.

It creates a bond between people that doesn't end with them. It is joyfully passed from then on to all who share in the connection of a quality meal. A skill passed on is a seed to grow that will one day nourish, entertain, or even change future generations. I fondly recall learning from Eileen the details of crafting the French omelet, and testing if spaghetti is ready by throwing it against the wall. These are the little things I hope to pass down, just as she did to me from her mother. Life derives meaning when shared, and food is a primary example of this.

I throw chopped onions and mushrooms into the mix once the bottom of the sprouts are black and charred, giving them a sweet, earthy taste. The telltale sign of a family recipe is a piece of paper that's time-worn and barely legible. More likely, the paper doesn't exist. The best family recipes are passed from the sincere words of the teacher to the open ears of the apprentice; they live only in sweet-smelling memories. While I'm far from a master, I can hold my own in the kitchen and improvise when I have to. I'm lost in my favorite music and the pops and sizzling sounds. It's a time to have fun and be myself without needing to follow a recipe. The chicken is baking with tomatoes and spices, and a brown crust forms. The scent wafting throughout the apartment smells delicious.

As I get older, I realize how important food can be to creating meaningful relationships, whether I'm a stranger in a foreign place or visiting home for the holidays. Nourishing food represents the character of one's heart in ways that words often can't, as cooking for somebody means you care about them. Cooking has provided a connection between people for hundreds of thousands of years.[42] The relationship created through food is no different now than it was when our ancestors huddled around the sway of a dancing flame.

I imagine an ancient dwelling, where the walls were dimly lit by a smoldering fire in the center of the room. Weapons and hides hung alongside dreams portrayed through the world's first paintings. Now, our pictures line the walls and what we collect reflects our personalities. Still, it's food that makes a house a home and brings us together no matter what species we are or what holiday it is.[43] Food provides us with a feeling of community and a sense of belonging.

I could be anywhere in the world, but I'm in Forks using the skills passed down from my family to create something meaningful, a memory, an emotion, a feeling of hope. I feel at home here in this kitchen—I have all I need. After dinner, I go through the day's photos and write a few notes in my journal. I fall asleep with the window open, listening to the sound of steady rain.

COCKADOODLE DOOOO! COCKADOODLE DOOOO! *You gotta be kidding.* It's 3:15 a.m. I wake from a strange dream. The details immediately fade. I was in a canyon; I've imagined it before. It's eerily similar to reality but different in uncanny ways that I can't put into words. I was with my hometown friends, Shaan, Adam, and Jordan.

We were looking through old video games, the ones you had to blow on like a harmonica to get to work. I miss those guys; I miss going out to parties and wondering how we'd get a thirty rack of beer. It took all week and earnest planning to figure out a way. I miss not worrying about money or goals or any of the things that keep me up at night. In high school, I had a particular set of worries, but they were no more real or illusory than those I have today. I've just learned to deal with them differently.

I take out my journal and turn on the dim bedside lamp. If I can't go to sleep because of a nagging thought, I must write it down. To abide by this rule, I leave my journal by my bed; I won't give myself an excuse not to write.

COCKADOODLE DOOO! *Really?* Every hour on the hour, the rooster outside crows. I laugh at the absurdity of the situation as I lay in bed. Let it go—the goals, the worry, and the angst. Let it all just fade away. Laugh at the sunrise song of the singing rooster.

I realize that I'm here because I'm following my dream; I get the same joy now from doing this as I did from playing video games as a kid. This is a video game, except instead of slicing through the forests of *Zelda*, I find myself lost in the towering Redwoods; instead of scaling the snow-capped mountains of *Skyrim*, I'm navigating Olympic; I'm on my hero's journey.

Writing always makes me feel better. It's as if the paper by my bed is the bridge between my dream state and the waking state, between my beating heart and my restless soul. I lay up in bed and think for a moment. The light from the living room falls through the door. It's cold in the room from the open window. The sound of the rain is soothing as I wrap myself in the comforter like a cocoon. Half asleep, I pour my dreams onto the page.

ARROWS OF YOUTH; THE EARLY STAGES

FORKS, WASHINGTON

Down, But Never Out

I know sometimes it feels as
Though you've nothing
Left to give,
That's when you dig
Your heels in,
There's much more life to live.
You may be hurting deep inside,
Not knowing where to turn,
But you're a fighter, always been,
The fire in you burns.
We've all been knocked down,
Caked in dust,
Our heart's been split asunder,
But you're the one who gets
Back up, a force as
Strong as thunder.
Life will often not make sense, no
Writing on the wall,
No truths lay hidden,
Rocks unturned,

You feel you've searched them all.
For answers written in the sky,
The wispy clouds of white,
You wish to join the birds aloft,
Life's easier in flight.
The heart within a soaring bird,
It knows not earthly pain,
But with our struggles,
Lessons rise,
Something to always gain.
Adversity will come to those with
Minds prepared to fight,
With every step,
Your aching limbs,
They move with greater might.
You take your shot, won't be held
Down, committed to the game,
Keep showing up, you're still
Right here;
You know you're not the same.

18
HOH RIVER TRAIL

MOUNT OLYMPUS IS A SIGHT TO BEHOLD ON THIS frosty winter's day. It serves as a central, snowy anchor point in the Olympic Peninsula. From a bird's-eye view it looks like it could be grabbed and broken off like the corner of a chocolate bar. Today I'm hiking the Hoh River Trail in the Hoh Rainforest, one of the largest temperate rainforests in the United States. I read a comment online about the trail being muddy. A hike in winter through a rainforest is muddy? *Come on, people.*

The damn rooster continues to crow every hour. Apparently that's how it wards off potential threats; I'm turning into an imminent threat after about five hours of this crowing. I make a hearty bowl of oatmeal for breakfast and head outside to load my car. There's a layer of delicate ice crystals coating the car's exterior. I run my hand through the frost and draw a smiley face. :) This is the first snow of the trip; the surround-

Arrows of Youth

ing fields have all turned white. I couldn't make out the neighborhood in last night's darkness, but now I see the chicken coop behind the owner's home. Yesterday I stood on the turbulent seashore. Now I'm in the mountains, running my hands through the snow. The snow on the ground vanishes with the rising sun. The air feels crisp and clean. It clears my mind with every inhale and courses through my veins.

Okay, rooster, I'm willing to make amends. This farm is my home as well. It's too lovely out not to be in a cheerful mood. With my adventure gear in tow, I get in my car and go. It takes about an hour to get to the Hoh River Trail through the winding roads of Washington. As I drive along the two-lane highway, I pass bare deciduous trees; others that keep their leaves are red, green, and purple. Something is happening to me after spending a few weeks in the arms of nature. I have but one focus every day, and that's enjoying it. Without somewhere to rush off to or a deadline to meet or plans to remember, I dance through the day and accommodate whatever experience arises at the moment. I want to live this way forever. As Jordan Peterson says, something is changing in my biology after waking each day with a single purpose of embracing the novel experience of being alive.

I approach the trail and drive along the rushing Hoh River toward Mount Olympus. The river serves as a passage from the icy blue glaciers down to the sea, like the intricate blue veins of our body that convey essential nutrients from the heart. Leonardo da Vinci wrote of the Earth as it compares to the human body, especially the ocean, which he considered the heart that sustains the rest of the planet. Leonardo wrote in his notebooks:[44]

The body of the Earth, like the bodies of animals, is interwoven with ramifications of veins, which are all joined together and are formed for the nutrition and vivification of the Earth and of its creatures. Its flesh is the soil, its bones are the arrangements of the connections of the rocks of which the mountains are composed. Its blood is the veins of waters; the lake of the blood, which is throughout the heart, is the ocean; its breathing and the increase and decrease of the blood through the pulses in the earth is thus: it is the flow and ebb of the sea.

Like the human body that Leonardo da Vinci passionately studied, everything about the world intertwines. I park and set off into the lively rainforest; there's a sheen on all the plants and trees, but it isn't raining. The forest is bursting with Sitka Spruce trees and Western Hemlocks, cedars, maples, and cottonwoods. The features of the Earth, the creatures, and humans—we are one environment in flux. In fact, there's much we can learn from the simplest life forms on this planet.

There's a ubiquitous layer of verdant green mosses and lichens covering every square inch of the forest. They provide nutritious food for the animals that call this rainforest home. But when they're not being eaten, the lichens just want to be. For a lichen, any additional time spent in the forest is winning at the game of life. Bill Bryson writes in *A Short History of Nearly Everything*:

It is easy to overlook this thought that life just is. As humans we are inclined to feel that life must have a point. We have plans and aspirations and desires. We want to take constant advantage of all the intoxicating existence we've been endowed with. But what's life to a lichen? Yet its impulse to exist, to be, is every bit as strong as ours—arguably even stronger. If I were told that I had to spend decades being a furry growth on a rock in the woods, I believe I would lose the will to go on. Lichens don't. Like virtually all living things, they will suffer any hardship, endure any insult, for a moment's additional existence. Life, in short, just wants to be.

I duck under reaching branches to walk along the clear, icy river. The white water rushes and congeals in glassy pools. Mount Olympus and a plethora of snow-capped mountains loom in the distance. I use them as my visual guide and begin gnawing on some jerky as I walk along the river. I cross several boggy bridges over creeks that cascade through the trees. What must it have been like for explorers back in the day? Now I can look online and find any trail in the area rated by its difficulty. I wonder if that's taken the serendipitous joy out of stumbling upon something like Yosemite Valley or turning a corner and unknowingly gazing upon Mount Olympus.

What would it be like to be an explorer and awake on a cold, refreshing morning? To pack up camp and head for the ocean or the mountains? Days would presumably comprise stalking game, listening to the sounds of birds, and studying the moss on trees to know in which direction to turn.

218

Perhaps it's up to us to retain that childlike spirit of adventure. Sometimes it's best to forgo the research beforehand. *Just go.*

I STOP TO ADMIRE A SLIVER of light that breaks through the branches of a tree. A soft rain begins to fall; it doesn't make a sound. A gentle rain is omnipresent, even on the sunniest of days. I watch the rain particles fall through the fragment of light. There's a small, translucent maple leaf hanging from the thread of a delicate twig. The light shines through the leaf; from its stem hangs a single raindrop in the shape of a diamond.

Even in this tranquil moment, my mind returns with questions, as forever a formidable foe. *Who are you doing this for? Who are you trying to impress?* Hardly a day goes by when I don't wonder: *What would Duke think? What would he do?* Much of the time, this is positive. He's always been my greatest role model, my best friend, and my older brother. Even though I'm the younger brother, I was thought of as the responsible sibling.

Like many younger brothers, perhaps I'd seen the conflict between my brother and my parents, and I just wanted peace. The first-born usually have to find their own way from a young age. He found what he loved—soccer, then surfing, then being a part of a big university, then acting. He underwent challenging times to reconcile positive relationships with my mom and Eileen. From my perspective, he felt he didn't have an escape. His high school friends weren't truly there for him. When I came into my own group of friends, I felt his pain.

I want nothing but the best for my friends; I love every one of them and harbor no jealousy. If one of us succeeds, we all succeed. I'll do

Arrows of Youth

everything I can to help them grow in their own ways. I've always felt the same way about Duke, yet as kids there's an innate sibling rivalry. It's in our biology, not to mention the stories that have shaped our culture like the Old Testament story of Cain and Abel. Many times I certainly filled my role as the conniving younger brother.

"What is this bag of beer doing under the bed?" My mom stormed into the living room. I could feel the heat welling up in my face. I was working on a fun bag, full of one-off beers and those taken home from the end of a party. They were warm, sandy and safely hidden under my brother's bed. *Damn, I was heartless.*

"It's Duke's!" I made it up. I lied. He was blamed. I still question why I did it. Perhaps this is why honesty is something I now care so deeply about. I hurt my brother and threw him under the bus. At this point I can't imagine lying, not to myself, and not to others. I've always wanted Duke to succeed. In high school, I hated if people would talk behind his back. I hated myself if I went along with it. I felt I had to be there for him if others weren't; that hasn't changed, but who he surrounds himself with has. After Duke graduated from SMU, he spent a year pursuing his master's degree at Bristol Old Vic Theatre School in Bristol, England.

Still, his search to find people who truly cared for him had become no easier. It looked like he had it all, but I knew how he must have hurt on the inside. He battled his own inner demons across the pond; he jumped through the fire and slew the dragon. I've seen what he's overcome; he's taken off his mask. When he should have been expressing his individuality, he sought to fit in, just as we all do at a young age. As he broke away from caring what others thought, he changed. But in reality,

I believe he accepted who he is—*a light*—an inspired soul. I constantly find myself wondering what he would do in any given situation. He does the moral thing, and he lives to encourage others, even if that means just making them laugh.

There are things we don't entirely agree on, even if they're not specified. But there's so much about life that we agree on wholeheartedly. His perspective, advice, and approval mean more to me than anybody else's. Still, as the younger brother, I have to pave my own path; this is for me, it isn't for Duke. I love my brothers Duke and Jesse more than anything. While we're a team and I'll be there for them at the drop of a hat, each of us must find our own way in the world. I'm doing this for me. This period must be strange for my younger brother Jesse; high school feels so important when it's all you know. Instead of trying to remember so much arbitrary knowledge, perhaps we can learn from the great masters like Leonardo da Vinci and teach kids simply to be curious about how the world really works.

You're told to aim high, get good grades, go to a prestigious college, and make something of yourself. Yet, as I'm just discovering what I'm passionate about in my mid-twenties, I wonder if I could have relaxed more, enjoyed the journey, and appreciated every step. Perhaps we can take a cue from the lichens—*every moment we're alive is winning at the game of life, (just don't get eaten, which is quite possible, metaphorically).* Whether we're in high school, graduate school, or no school at all, each step has its purpose, and maybe that's simply to enjoy it, learn from it, and use it to grow.

I STUMBLE UPON A FIRE PIT ALONG THE RIVER, surrounded by a few saturated logs. I've walked for about four miles. Across the river, the trees look like they've been dusted with powdered sugar. After a few rows of trees without snow, those above are powdered and white. I sit on a log and pull out a sandwich with peanut butter and local jam I picked up from Yosemite. The sandwich is slightly frozen, as are my hands. I open up the gluey top and place beef jerky inside. *I'm living my best life.*

The first bite is delicious; I was confident it would be. A mist permeates through the trees on both sides of the river and envelopes the forest. The snowy mountains in the distance disappear and the sky becomes a diminished dark blue, like the color of the distant ocean. I pull out my journal and attempt to illustrate the scene, but it's difficult to write with my hands so cold. All I strive to do is capture the memory; a few words are all it takes. *Icy river. Misty forest. Snow dusted like sugar. Beef jerky in the peanut butter sandwich.* Perfect.

I begin my descent back along the river. My pants and my shoes are delightfully muddy and I'm sure I smell pungent. I love what I've created, the thoughts inside my head, the environment I'm in, the outlook I foster. Yet I still think about how I compare myself to others. Why is this so natural for us as human beings? *Is there a right or wrong?* The chiming sounds of the forest provide a melody against which to think. Regardless, I'm here now and my spirit is high; it roars amongst the trees. It wants to get lost to find its way. I exit the rainforest and return to my car in time to catch the golden sun retreating behind the far peaks. I drive along the Hoh River listening to jazz as the trees turn black and the river shimmers. It's another magical dusk.

When Pain Befalls Like Snow

Which way are we
Supposed to turn
When pain befalls like snow,
Our hope begins to fade away,
The path we've come to know?

Difficulties make time pause
A river comes to freeze,
We take the chance to look around,
And notice sleeping trees.

Usually, life flows like water
Clean enough to drink,
Then come the frost
And numbing ice,
To make us stop and think.
As fresh snow falls
We use our strength

To make it one more day,
No sounds to hear
But our heartbeat,
There's nothing left to say.

A season new
We've made it through,
The winter comes and goes.
Solid no more
Unlike before,
The water drowns our woes.

Each season holds its mysteries
The hurt will fall like snow,
But fight until we
Feel new warmth,
The wounds ensure we grow.

19
THE MYSTERIES OF RIALTO BEACH

ICTURE THE UNITED STATES AS A PUZZLE. Olympic National Park would make up the pivotal cornerstone piece that holds it all together. Because of its size, I broke up my time in Olympic between Forks and Port Angeles, a better-known town in the park's northeast section. Port Angeles sits on one side of the Strait of Juan de Fuca. Across the water lies Vancouver Island, the first entry point into Canada beyond America's northwestern tip. On the way to Port Angeles I plan to stop at Rialto Beach, one of Olympic's must-see spectacles. The morning sun melts the frost that lingers on the ground, the subtle sign of night.

I pull into the parking lot after the short drive and prepare for the day, which I assume will be defined by a couple of hours of hiking. I pack my camera and lunch and my yellow puffy jacket. The first thing I notice when I step onto the sand are the trees along the beach. They

Arrows of Youth

look like the spiny skeletons of devoured fish. Most are bereft of leaves, and their branches are erect as arrows. I begin my journey down the beach, trudging through the sand with little of a plan.

Like a favorite hat or a faithful owl, they say a truly great walking stick finds its master. I've searched over land, mountains, and rivers. I'm shocked that I still haven't found a reliable walking stick. From a distance, I can tell that the search has finally ended. Along the shore are piles of sticks and wood reminiscent of ancient catacombs filled to the brim with decaying bones. That's not where I find the stick. It's off by itself, beckoning the opportune wielder. I haven't asked for this, but the signs are clear. It's nimble, dexterous, and sturdy. It's dry, yet full of life from its time at sea. I pick up the stick, and like Harry Potter uniting with his wand, the stick becomes a part of me.

There aren't any people around, save an older couple heading in the same direction. Their unified demeanor puts a smile on my face. The man looks like my high school biology teacher, akin to a walrus with big silvery whiskers and seasoned, dark eyes. The woman wears a pair of dainty glasses on the tip of her nose and a baggy grey hoodie. They look content with where they are, scouring the sand for stones. The woman goes off on her own with her head looking down as if she's lost her keys in the sand.

Rialto's centerpiece is a massive rock formation that projects from the sand like a whale's tooth split in twain. Rugged islands sprout from the water between the shore and the horizon and attract my gaze when I look into the sun. I wonder what it must have been like for Native Americans to paddle out and explore the forests that dwell atop the islands. What mysteries might they contain?

It appears there's nowhere else to go, but I have trouble believing this is the end of the line. A wall of stone stands in my way, but what lies on the other side? I head into the forest to look around. Lo and behold, I come across a dilapidated, hidden set of stairs leading over the rocks. They're covered in leaves and branches and are easy to miss. I climb the stairs and from the top I view the entire cove I just traversed. Yet, it's what lies on the other side that blows me away. A whole other cove unfurls for several miles of stony beach. Nobody's there. To conceal my location, I look back to see if anybody's watching.

I make my way through the sappy trees and am back on the sand; I notice a cave at the tip of the rock I just scaled. It's a perfect oval hole about twenty feet high. It may have been underwater just thirty minutes before—I'm positive it wasn't there. Rialto Beach feels like the last frontier of land and sea. Rocks, boulders, and fallen trees all meet here at this great northwestern threshold. Salmon ride the rivers like highways from the mountains to the ocean, then come back to the rivers to lay eggs where they were born. Then, they die honorably. I cross one of these flowing rivers by utilizing a fallen tree that serves as a bridge for those willing to take the risk of falling in. It's slippery; I walk across like I'm treading a tightrope. *Don't overthink it.*

I hike to the furthest cove I can access and sit down on one of the dry logs. The wind is cold, but the sun shining down on my skin feels brilliant. I close my eyes and listen to the sound of the birds squawking all around me. The gentle sound of the ocean ebbing and flowing against the shore makes me pensive. After spending the past couple of weeks in constant movement, I close my eyes and slip away.

HOLE-IN-THE-WALL CAVE; RIALTO BEACH

OVER THE LAST SEVERAL YEARS, I've battled a back injury that has taken away my freedom to exercise, an integral facet of my identity. I do everything I can to ensure the pain doesn't take over my life, but it's provided my greatest challenge to date. It happened almost four years ago. My lower disc sprained or ruptured or slipped while working out; I haven't been able to find confidence in an answer.

When I open my eyes early in the morning, the first thing I ask is *How does my back feel?* Often, it's not good. The pain in my lower back, the side of my hips, the front of my hips, and even my entire upper back, often makes it feel like I'm a walking stack of spinning plates where if one slips the entire thing will come crashing down. Still, I use my mental fortitude to put on a cheerful face and act like everything is okay. I tell myself I have to be strong. Sometimes I want to give up and scream "THIS FUCKING SUCKS!" as loud as I can. That's the thing about pain. No matter what it is, when we feel pain it's impossible to think about anything else. We're bound by the pain when it infiltrates our mind; our known universe becomes confined to that pain. I've tried to fight it.

This has sent me down the road of despair because I couldn't get past my mind or my body. I've approached the injury from the physical; I've seen countless professionals who have thrown their hands up in bafflement. *My injury beat them, but it hasn't beaten me.* I'm done fighting. I need to do the spiritual work to let go of anything that doesn't serve my current self. The fear—what is fear? I've been angry that I can't logically fix this part of me; I don't know what to do. The breath brings me into my body; I want it to heal. I want it to know that I surrender; the fight is over. I acknowledge the pain. I feel it.

What do I need to let go of? What is it that my body needs to tell me? I've tried to strengthen it, but the injury has always come back when I've thought I escaped its grasp. Tears fall from my eyes when I feel like a part of me needs to release, but I don't know what it's holding on to. I've cried many times over the years, yet in the last several months I've cried practically on a weekly basis. It's not because it hurts any more than it ever has. I've gone into the pain and have reached a lovingness for myself that doesn't need to attach to my past identity. I've gone inward to find out what it is I need to let go of. I'm still uncertain; but my goal each day is to seek it out peacefully. More often than not I'm playing basketball, soccer, tennis, golf, or lacrosse in my dreams. I'm on the pitch under the lights, sprinting at full speed, dribbling a ball, shooting, and smiling with my friends. I wake up in a cold sweat and make a subtle move to feel if the pain's still there. It is.

Without the injury, I would not be who I am today. The pain has provided me with purpose. I wouldn't feel the same gratitude for life's simple pleasures, such as walking with my own two legs and seeing with my own two eyes. I have so much, and this is what I must brave. The pain won't take away my freedom of thought, my freedom of choice, or my freedom to see each day as a gift. The day will come when I'm pain free. This has happened to me for a reason. I will continue to grow and continuously fight every day that I'm alive, even if that only means letting go. I've sought the answers from the exterior world, but perhaps I've been looking in the wrong place. My focus has been healing my body, but I realize it likely won't happen in the way I expect.

"When I run after what I think I want,

My days are a furnace of distress and anxiety;

If I sit in my own place of patience,

What I need flows to me, and without any pain.

From this I understand that what I want also wants me,

Is looking for me and attracting me.

There is a great secret in this for anyone who can grasp it."[45]

– *Rumi*

If I sit in my own place of patience, what I need flows to me, and without any pain. I've been pondering these lines and allow them to take control of my being. Often we look for the answers to life's most mysterious questions in the exterior world. We're constantly searching, seeking, and moving. But sometimes all I want to do is sit for a while without striving to find the answer. I close my eyes to travel within, past the physical and the mental. Daily practices such as this help me get in touch with my spirit, the part of me that, perhaps, I watch roll away in the shimmering surf. We all foster a boundless spirit, yet we're seldom told how to connect with it. The spirit is our essence that doesn't attach to any feeling, any thought, any dream or goal or aim. Uncovering our spirituality provides more meaning than the physical and the mental can.

While connecting with our spiritual self is a lifelong pursuit, I've found a more profound sense of meaning in who I am and what I want out of life.

The body is an extraordinary thing, but it has its limitations. The heart that beats within my chest is generated from processes that weave through all of time, incomprehensible to fathom in their scope. Our body is of the soil; we are of the earth. Like the body, the mind is unique to each individual yet runs deeper than any well. Our thoughts, emotions, and everyday actions derive from the depths of our minds. The French philosopher René Descartes famously said:

"I think, therefore I am."[46]

What we're able to conceive with our mind becomes our reality. We think, and then we do. We draw upon our memory and combine that information with what we think we know—but what do we really know? The same mind that tells us how the world works, at its worst, tells us we're not good enough, not pretty enough, or not smart enough. Minutes later, it tries to make amends. Who or what is our mind made of? We can train the mind to be our greatest asset and motivator, but that takes tireless, conscious effort, day in and day out. Yet, if we're going to do anything with this life, training our own mind is of utmost importance.

We don't determine what happens *to* us in life. Yet our mind determines how we react, if we react at all. To see the world as against us or for us; to see each setback as a blessing or a failure; that's the decision for the mind to make. For the mind, there's always something to figure out and protect. We must foster a profound sense of being to quiet the mind and make it our friend. *Being*—that is what we already are. Our spirit is the facet of us that exists in unyielding love. There's another way to look at the famous Descartes axiom from the Indian mystic Sadhguru. He wrote in his book *Inner Engineering: A Yogi's Guide to Joy:*[47]

> *It is only because you exist that you can generate a thought. It is time to restate a fundamental fact: you are, therefore you may think. The most beautiful moments in your life—what you might consider moments of bliss, joy, ecstasy, or utter peace— were moments when you were not thinking about anything at all. You were just being. Even without your thoughts, existence is.*

The spiritual is our reason for existence. Through spiritual pursuits such as meditation and deep breathing, we transcend the rational body or the contemplative mind. The spirit is being itself in the purest sense of the word, yet words are clumsy tools. It doesn't matter what we're doing in the physical world; if our spirit's at peace and in tune with the natural flow of life, our mind and body will follow. I don't know what it might take, but I long to get there, because in the moments when I feel something beyond the physical and the mental, life becomes effortless.

I used to find it hard to believe that what we think controls our physical body and that our emotional baggage can literally weigh us down. But right now and forevermore, I'm devoted to opening up my heart and going where I've never been. There's tremendous joy in realizing we don't need to push ourselves constantly. There's freedom in letting go of the exterior pursuit of perfection. I'm seeking a way in. I have to listen—enough fighting, enough searching—just listen to what the world and that inner voice, *not my mind*, but my soul, is telling me.

Nothing about our existence is mundane; there's magic all around us and there's life, unexplainable life, taking place within our bodies. Everything's connected; the way we move through the day determines how we move through life; how we treat ourselves is how we treat other human beings. We don't need to search for love. We are love. We don't need to search for meaning. We are meaning. Often we're so focused on doing, fixing, and growing that we forget what it's like to sit in patience, *waiting*.

Doing has a start and a finish. But when one thing is done we move on to the next without considering the importance of what we've done. There's a profound level of peace in waiting and being okay with it. It's not expecting something to change in the physical world, nor grinding away to get to some goal we don't connect with. It's existing in the world in a way that only we can, where pain will wash away, where suffering will cease, and where meaning will flourish. The pain has brought me here; for that I'm infinitely grateful. The pain has brought me in; I know it's for a reason.

In the words of Rumi: *What I want also wants me, is looking for me and attracting me.* In this moment, all I want to do is listen to the waves and let go of the pain. What's out of our control dictates our lives when we believe life will get better when something *out there* changes. Once I find the right person, change jobs, lose weight, or finally heal, then I'll be happy. We all battle this paradigm every day, but it's not a battle worth fighting. Liberation comes from letting go and focusing on the only thing we can control—our minds. We can turn our mind into our greatest ally, our most trusted friend, and our savior by living every day in gratitude.

Arrows of Youth

Life will always put challenges in front of us, but our inner world mustn't be determined by what's taking place outside. I feel deep within my bones that this period of my life is happening for a crucial reason. I choose to be grateful. I choose to see beauty. I choose deathless love for myself and the world, today and always. I took this trip to prove to myself that my circumstances won't hold me back—not the constraints of my body or my mind. I've made it; I'm here. Now I just let time fade away. I lay back on the fallen tree and relish in the sound of silence.

I OPEN MY EYES TO FALLING STONES coming from the cliff behind me. I get up and move and take a long, panoramic look around. It's almost dusk; there is no wind and the tide has dropped. It's as if the tide has unearthed an underwater, cavernous city. From this vantage point at the tip of the beach, the landscape is nothing short of magnificent in every direction I look. Lush trees line the beach and islands dot the coastline as if they're kids, breaking away from home to make it on their own.

People populate the beach as sunset nears. I head back, yet I stop to walk amongst the tide pools near the hole-in-the-wall cave. I'm about a quarter-mile beyond the cave, out at sea, hopping from one rocky, pink, mollusk-covered formation to the next. The minty green sea anemones appear alien in color and form.

We live on an alien rock. These creatures live beneath the sea's surface; they're green and have tentacles surrounding a gaping hole. And we worry about how we look in yoga pants. We worry about whether our eyebrows are unkempt, what that person thinks about us, or if we'll ever be free from pain. Yet we live amongst aliens; we are aliens. It's almost comical to see these creatures; they make me realize how strange life is. All we can do is laugh and savor every second of our time on this floating rock.

I watch the water gather in the tide pools and reverberate through the irregular formations. Minuscule waves emanate from a central pool and I can't help but think of da Vinci. He scrupulously studied the water eddies forming in Florence's River Arno and constantly contemplated the fluid element's movement. Leonardo watched the world work; this gave him profound meaning. As the planet moved, so did his impassioned mind; he wanted to explain the way things are. This passion brought him joy, just as it does me. The micro-waves emanating from the pools look like flowing glass, and reach the surrounding rocks and dissolve like dust.

A bird, possibly an eagle, flies atop the tree line. There's a man working on a fire next to a hatched tent. The fire gives off a reassuring glow and a delicious, smoky smell. We're all just children out here, exploring, watching, and listening; I'm learning what it means to let go and be, just as much as the curious golden retriever on the beach. We are all connected. If we stop moving and sit in our own place of patience, what we need will flow to us, and with no pain. What we need is a connection to one another and a oneness with this alien rock we call home. Olympic is like nowhere I've ever experienced in the world.

Arrows of Youth

I Know That I've Been Here Before

I know that I've been here before,
Cold ocean water, a book,
An empty page.
My mind is clear though
Full of thoughts,
Sea foam breaks softly
On the shore.
What else does one need, but the
Things which make us happy?
I leave to think,
Surrounded by nature's breath,
The winds of changing seasons.
The more I climb, I ponder time,
I know that I've been here before.
Step after step brings clarity;
These days, that's all I seek.
This day resembling others,
This feeling not brand new,
We search for that which
Makes us full,

No less than that will do.
To be young with life before me,
I have all that I need.
Health, love, a beating heart,
A soul that longs to speak.
Each season brings its loveliness,
The planet floats,
As does the spirit,
Looking for connection.

Is that enough to fill the heart,
A life of simplicity?
I hope it is,
I know I can,
Find sheer joy in what's not new.

I know that I've been here before,
And that is all I need.
All that I love is with me now,
A life of simplicity.

20

STORM KING

THE SOMNOLENCE OF THE WINTER NIGHT has me struggling to stay awake as I drive through downtown Port Angeles. After I pick up groceries, I head into the neighboring hills to find where I'll be staying. Practically every house twinkles with Christmas lights. Many have full Christmas displays set up in their driveways; they're almost too much. *Almost*. It takes two laps around the neighborhood to find the address of my Airbnb.

The charming blue cottage sits on the street corner; I pull past the chain-link fence into the driveway. It's been peculiar pulling into random driveways. It's a strange feeling at first, to have no clue what to expect. The owner doesn't know who I am; to them, I'm just a guy coming to stay for a few days. There's something fascinating about it—a mutual trust to uphold. This is a home just like where I grew up, although it's in a part of the world I've never been to with people I didn't know existed

Arrows of Youth

until now. Not personally, anyway. Life carries on and we think about our own worlds, but now I'm a part of somebody else's.

As I'm unpacking the car, the owner comes outside to greet me. Two small pigtails hold up his greying hair. Evidently he's confident and pulls it off. He wears a black t-shirt with no jacket. I imagine the feeling of running out into the cold, yet his face shows no sign of worry; I can see his sons and wife seated and laughing at the dinner table through the window, and hear the joyful sounds of a tight-knit family: clinking kitchenware and muffled conversation. His relaxed demeanor and quirky smile tell me he has all he needs, right there with him. I tell him about the trip so far and describe the calmness of Rialto Beach and the Hoh Rainforest, as well as the raw power of the sea at Ruby Beach. I feel sincere gratitude for telling a local how much I admire their home.

"Well, if you have no plans for tomorrow," he says with his arms nonchalantly folded—*is he not freezing?*—"you should go to Seattle."

"Whoa," I reply, mid-consideration. I hadn't thought about it, but it's a tempting idea. Seattle is about two and a half hours if I take a ferry across Puget Sound, and three hours if I drive around through Tacoma, Washington. But do I want to see Seattle by myself while everything is closed? My dad and I have always talked about visiting Seattle together. The city checks off our holy trinity of childhood travel: football, rain, and delicious food. I'll get there with him soon; it will be worth saving.

"Anyway, think about it," he says after he can see me knocking the idea around in my noggin for a few seconds.

"There are eggs, butter, and cream from our farm in the studio's fridge. Let me know if you need anything else!"

"That's amazing, thank you." It's quite a welcome. He ambles back inside the warmth of his home. I grab my things from the car and look inside the studio. Wood boards make up the entire walls. The details of the space are copper and metallic. It's minimalist and has a rustic winter style that makes me smile from ear to ear. There's the subtle smell of sweet pine coming from a Christmas wreath hanging on the wall. One wall has a small wooden desk against it with a metal box of vinyl sitting on the ground below.

I pull out an album by The Beatles and delicately place it on the record player. Music—it can turn any situation into a party. Songs are an expression of emotion through a few words and a melody. With my heart full of music this feels like home—the type of home Henry David Thoreau lived in for two years by Walden Pond, the type of place I'd love to call my own. Thoreau didn't have a record player or a minimalist kitchen in his cabin, however. Still, I feel the connection to Thoreau; I strive to appreciate nature with the same fundamental awe as he portrays in *Walden*,[48] a book that sincerely changed how I perceive the natural world.

Walden tells of Thoreau's two years during the 1840s living in the forest close to Concord, Massachusetts, on the land of fellow nineteenth-century transcendentalist Ralph Waldo Emerson. Thoreau writes:

> *I went to the woods because I wished to live deliberately, to front only the essential facts of life, and see if I could not learn what it had to teach, and not, when I came to die, discover that I had not lived.*

Arrows of Youth

It seems nature provided Thoreau with an eternal ember blazing in his soul, as he, along with another of my greatest inspirations, Leonardo da Vinci, found meaning by marveling at the way the world works. Thoreau appears a simple man, keen on stripping life down to the bare necessities and living every day with a dynamic spirit. He was a man freely against conformity; he sought to find what lit his soul on fire. Thoreau has inspired me to recognize that our perspective shapes our reality. We choose if that reality is beautiful not only with our eyes, but our entire being. Thoreau writes:

> *It is something to be able to paint a particular picture, or to carve a statue, and so to make a few objects beautiful; but it is far more glorious to carve and paint the very atmosphere and medium through which we look, which morally we can do. To affect the quality of the day, that is the highest of arts. Every man is tasked to make his life, even in its details, worthy of the contemplation of his most elevated and critical hour.*

What is life, if not beautiful? What are we really striving for? From an open sky to a simple, comforting home, beauty turns our every day into something more, something nearly divine. To act morally and righteously to one another and share in the gift of life is just as beautiful as a perfect *Starry Night*. I take a hot shower and read *Eragon* after making some dinner. The pattering sound of rain falling against the roof puts me right to sleep.

IT'S ALL IN THE DETAILS

THE MORNING IS CHILLY; the sky is blue as a bird. A few plumes of clouds gently float by. Now that it's light out, I poke around the backyard of this quintessential family farmhouse. A white sheet hangs by a thin wire and blows in the wind above a few chickens. They step lethargically across the small green yard. Dark red berries and pale green pears hang from vines in the garden. I go back into my dojo, put water in the boiler, and beans in the coffee grinder. I grind the beans into a powder as the water heats, then pour them into the French press. I fill the container with the boiling water and watch the effervescent chemical reaction as the coffee brews.

The liquid looks like the soil outside and smells like chocolate earth. I pull out two eggs from the farm and crack them into a pan while simmering some oatmeal. The morning staple, oatmeal à la Vincent, is on the way. When the oatmeal is ready, I put in the fresh berries, peanut butter, nuts, and an egg on top. The egg is salty and crispy, and when I break into it, the yolk slowly soaks into the oats.

The plan for the day is to check out a hot spring about an hour away. I pack up and head out once I know how to get there. As I sit in my car with the engine on, I look up the hot spring one more time to make sure it's doable. The clear blue morning has turned into a substantial rain.

The website reads: *Road washed away. Closed.* It's a tough call to make. These online reviews are utterly ridiculous about 70 percent of the time. The comments say these hot springs smell bad, a rainforest hike is muddy, and a path along a river is monotonous. I wonder if I can trust these reviews to plan my day. I'm in my swim trunks sitting in the car, watching smoke rise from the exhaust to vanish into the Washington air. It's not worth it. Time for a change of plan.

I go back inside and put hiking pants on. I decide I'll save Seattle for another trip. I look into Marymere Falls, a one-and-a-half-mile round-trip hike. That sounds mellow in what is now pouring rain. I make some Sencha green tea and bring it with me in a canister. I'm just going to go.

I GET A CALL FROM MORGAN. He's in Carmel, a quaint town in Northern California that's home to the world-class Pebble Beach Golf Course. When Morgan and I graduated from high school, we spent two nights at Pebble Beach with our dads as a graduation present. It was the first time I smoked a cigar and drank champagne with my best friend *and our dads.* Who gets to experience something like that as a high school graduate? It was one of the first times I saw my dad and John, Morgan's dad, as our friends.

"Hey buddy, I'm at Carmel-by-the-Sea!" Just hearing Morgan's voice puts me in a great mood. We don't even need anything to laugh about; we just start laughing hysterically. "I'm about to play the Pebble back-nine," he says in the sarcastic dialogue we speak in more often than coherent sentences anybody would understand.

"I think they should remember you from our graduation trip," I tell him through my semi-contained laughter.

"Yeah, they should let me just walk on." The price to play Pebble Beach is exorbitant. Sharing laughs on the legendary course is a celebration to remember for a lifetime, regardless if we sank a single putt. I had one or two.

"So, how's the gear been? How's the car doing?"

"It's all holding up well! The car is getting muddy, but that's part of it." I'm learning to love getting into the cold and muddy car; it's the sign of a day well spent. My attitude towards clothing and stuff has changed for the better over the last couple of years. I believe in simplifying and truly loving what I have. As a kid, I imagined I'd grow up and strive for a big house. I did not know how I'd get there. It's okay because now I'm after something different. I'm after the intangible, searching further within myself to discover what I'm made of.

Things can't provide meaning; while our things speak to who we are, they don't define us. Meaning comes from the inner spark that ignites when we're truly living, when the spirit within us is given a chance to breathe. Mark Manson's book *The Subtle Art of Not Giving a F*ck* [49] inspired me to be happy with less and to strive to simplify and focus on what's truly important. This goes for our material things and what we want out of life.

Finding what makes life worthwhile can be as straightforward or complicated as we make it. Often, it's doing less, wanting less, and caring about less that provides the greatest peace. This doesn't mean we have to stop being human. It means reflecting on what we genuinely love, so we may focus on that with the entirety of our being. As Mark Manson delicately puts it:

The world is constantly telling you that the path to a better life is more, more, more . . . The problem is that giving too many fucks is bad for your mental health. It causes you to dedicate your life to chasing a mirage of happiness and satisfaction. The key to a good life is not giving a fuck about more; it's giving a fuck about less, about only what is true and immediate and important.

There's meaning all around us, but it's not in things. Meaning comes from how we connect with the world and with others; it's how we change people's lives by being us. It's what I make of today and how my spirit works in harmony with what I have.

When I moved from Los Angeles to San Diego at the beginning of fall, giving away my things and decluttering was difficult, yet incredibly liberating. It's emotional to give our things away. We feel what we own is *ours*. We've worked for them, we've paid for them, and at one point, they've meant something special to us. Our things remind us of our memories; saying goodbye to them is letting go of the past. Yet, when an experience truly matters, the memory will always remain.

I used the move as a rewarding opportunity to simplify, declutter, and give away what I no longer needed. I also found it to be an opportunity to give away a few things I loved, too. There will always be more stuff in our lives. It's a valuable skill to get comfortable with less. When we give, we can only benefit from a clearer mind and a cleaner space. When we're able to say goodbye without wishing for anything in return, then giving benefits the giver as much as it does the receiver, as giving a piece of our heart to a stranger creates a kinship with the universe.

I'll never forget being in a grocery store in Tokyo with Morgan in 2019. We were checking out when the cashier recognized the Los Angeles skate brand, *Rip City Skates,* on his bright red hoodie. The cashier's eyes blossomed and his face flushed with excitement. Morgan noticed. He took his favorite sweatshirt off his back and gave it to the cashier. The man didn't know what to say. He was genuinely appreciative. Morgan left a piece of his heart on the other corner of the globe. He loved that sweatshirt, which made it more special to give away. I'll always remember Morgan's selfless gesture.

I now strive to use what I have and use it well. My things are reflections of me. I don't want to have new stuff all the time; I want to love what I have. When I look at my things, I want to remember the times I used them and the joy they brought me and will continue to bring. I'd rather have a sewn-up pair of pants from this trip than a fresh pair in two months. I want to look at this yellow puffer jacket and beam every time I think about its adventures.

THE MARYMERE FALLS HIKE starts at the base of Crescent Lake. There are hardly any people in the parking lot, just a couple at the end of a dock looking out into the steel-blue water. I expect a short hike, but the rain is coming down hard, so I grab my umbrella and put on my boots, ready for anything. I text Morgan: *Btw, a big part of the trip comes from what you told me about your grandpa in Germany. Didn't he say when getting into the Mercedes, the car is for us. We're not for the car? This has been my motto.*

He texts me back: *I think about that all the time! I didn't want to wear my white shoes in the mud today, but I thought of that line.* Our minds are on the same page. I take a moment to walk to the end of the dock and watch the rain piercing the water's surface. The lake, the sky, and the heavens above are all icy and grey and blend into one slate shade. I walk away from the lake, reveling in the sound of rain against my umbrella. I follow signs for Marymere Trail; they take me through a tunnel under the main road. At about a quarter of a mile in, I see another sign pointing left: *Storm King Trail.*

How could I not be inclined? I take the alternative route and, after a couple of minutes, understand why it's called Storm King. My thought is that the hike will take me to a spot high above the clouds where the rain ceases. I ascend like a mountain goat straight into the sky, marching uphill from switchback to switchback. This isn't a one-and-a-half-mile loop to a waterfall anymore. The day has shown me an unfamiliar path. I've taken it.

I hike through dense, minty green trees for about an hour with no viewpoints. It's step after step of trekking up red clay through mossy, electric trees that look zapped by lightning and glazed over from the cold. I pass a tree with a face that looks frozen in time. The tranquility of the forest, the endless rain, grabs a hold of my energy. I take a moment on a corner of a switchback to catch my breath and take off my jacket and beanie. *Genghis: Birth of an Empire* comes to mind as I hike the mountain of red clay. I'm in search of my eagle. I'm following my instincts and learning to trust myself. I didn't plan this hike, nor the best parts of this trip, which always seems to be the next one.

The sound of rain flowing through the trees is mesmerizing. This moment, walking up a mountain in the pouring rain, transcends time. It joins me with the humans of the past and all those that will come who take steps to reach their eagle.

The rain quiets. I look into the trees and can't tell if it's continuing to fall, but I can see the clouds have dissipated when I look up. I step through the last layer of ashen clouds and then suddenly, they're below me. The sound of rain breaks off altogether. Suddenly I'm next to a cliff's edge. I slowly inch and peer over. I made it. Down below is all that I climbed, the heavy clouds, and the opaque green trees. It's one of the most beautiful views I've ever seen. The clouds float above the very spot where I stood next to Crescent Lake a mere couple of hours earlier.

Water and ice envelope the world, yet I've crested that world below. I stand above on the edge of the cliff, watching, thinking, being. I ponder a quote from one of my favorite books, *Shogun*, by James Clavell.[50] The wise seventeenth-century Japanese samurai lord, Toranaga, thinks to himself:

> *"What shall I do? Nothing more than usual. Be patient, seek harmony, put aside all worries about I or thou, life or death, oblivion or afterlife, now or then, and set a new plan into motion."*

The serenity of the lake and the surrounding mountains overwhelms me. The natural elements harmonize in absolute majesty—the chaos of the day is below; above, silence. I stand on the edge of the cliff and find it difficult to leave. I just want to watch; patiently watch. There's a faint shining light in the clouds across the lake. This might as well be the gate to heaven.

I squat on the cliff and grab a handful of soft red clay. It feels good in my hand. It feels good to grab the earth, hold it, watch it crumble, and feel that I'm a part of it. I think of Oregon compared to where I now stand. I think of verdant green, sprawling fields, and golden light. Now I watch the purple sky darken as the mountain's shadow is cast across the lake. Two states, one land. Physically, the borders don't mean anything. I haven't driven from state to state; I've driven across a vast expanse of Earth that has changed drastically—from San Diego, where the mountains are sandy and the water is warm, to the peak of the Pacific Northwest, where the water is dark and rages, and the trees look like they have faces. I leave my vantage point and begin my descent down the mountain.

I still have time to check out Marymere Falls before the sun goes down. It's dusk, yet there's still just enough light to make it. I pick up the pace and reach the first bridge. I can hear the falls. The rushing water. The natural altering of the Earth. I follow the sound and cross another wooden bridge. The sound continues to get louder until finally I reach the falls. It's practically dark as the energy moves through me. I didn't expect this. The force flowing from the crashing water produces a constant misty wind that blows against my face. How can this sort of power exist and we hardly even know it's there? In this corner of the world—this pocket of wonder—life continues as it always has. In bearing witness, I feel I'm a part of something far greater than we'll ever know. We live amongst the result of a process billions of years in the making.

I go to bed smiling once again. Each day in Olympic National Park, I've woken up without knowing what the day would entail. Again, I fall

Arrows of Youth

asleep smiling, laughing, and overcome with reverence for the raw grandeur of our home, Earth.

O, Midnight Owl

What about the hoo'ing owl
Makes us think she's wise?
The way she's perched
On arms of trees,
Is it those big brown eyes?
The hoo is muffled, silent call,
No ostentatious claim,
We hear it under starry nights,
Alike the crackling flame.
Not one, not two,
But three parts hoo,
Have brought me out of sleep,
What have you seen,
O Midnight Owl,
Whose fellowship you keep?

Your life is lived
Amongst the trees,
With speed you burn through sky,

But now you're resting
By my home,
You've chosen not to fly.
And I commend you
For this pause,
It seems you've had your fill,
No longer soaring,
Eyes cast down,
Looking for mice to kill.
So what about the hoo'ing owl,
Makes us think she's wise?
Perhaps she spends time
Watching humans,
Noting our demise.
To be at night under the moon,
Not needing more to live,
Your subdued hoo
Has brought me joy,
Your gift of peace to give.

21
THE DOVE & OLIVE BRANCH

ESKOWIN, A MODEST BEACH TOWN on the Oregon Coast, lies about 340 miles southwest of Port Angeles. It's a stunning day that lures me out early in the morning. The clouds are dramatic and pronounced against the crisp, cerulean sky. The drive along the coast will take longer than if I took the major highway by a couple of hours. I opt for the longer route—what's a couple more hours? Jordan Peterson writes in *12 Rules for Life*:

> *To journey happily may well be better than to arrive*
> *successfully.*

I stop at a roadside espresso hut as I leave Port Angeles and begin another day on the road. Swaying trees and the lively sea pass me by, along with deteriorating general stores and coastal diners. My curiosity brought me here; I have a will to know what this life truly means to me. The most useful way I've been able to discern any answer is by observing nature; it continues to breathe, and this helps me breathe. Observing makes me realize that finding magic doesn't have to take more than watching. Still, I never stop wondering if there's more to our existence; life has become infinitely more meaningful as I've contemplated what is really taking place.

I consider what has had to occur across unfathomable spans of time to reach this point, where I'm driving a machine along the coast, pondering my place in the solar system and my own consciousness. We have a life inside of us that transpires simultaneously within the story of creation, history, and evolution. We're a part of something so inexplicable that our lives become trivial. The thought of what's possible, the thought of what we're perceiving, *life*, becomes too much to bear.

Maybe it takes stepping outside of our own human consciousness to realize what matters. There's always another question to be asked when we realize how little we know. Why do we abide by the social constructs that we do? Well, because they seem to work. Still, this doesn't mean they aren't in need of change. When we lose sight of the big picture, we focus on ourselves, the individual. When we focus only on our own problems, they blossom into unsurmountable challenges. We're confined to what we think we know. Yet when we accept ignorance we're able to grow, because then the possibilities are limitless. To study history is to inquire about how we've come to where we are and how we've spun this web of meaning. The rain comes down harder as I lose myself in thought. I watch the ocean go by, crashing and restless, like the human soul.

A BLUSTERY DAY ON THE OREGON COAST

I STARTED READING THE BIBLE for the first time in my life during the pandemic. As my fascination with history, philosophy, and spirituality has blossomed, I've felt a powerful urge to better understand this ancient text that serves as a cradle for Western civilization. I desire to formulate my own ideas regarding religion; to remain incognizant, at least of what the book actually entails, is a non-option. I seek to know what I truly believe. Jordan Peterson writes:

> *We've been watching ourselves act, reflecting on that watching, telling stories to still do that reflection, for tens and perhaps hundreds of thousands of years. That is all part of our attempts individual and collective to discover and articulate what it is that we believe. Part of the knowledge so generated is what is encapsulated in the fundamental teachings of our cultures and ancient writings such as the Tao Te Ching, the Vedic scriptures or the biblical stories.*

Just as I search for meaning in the world, the writers of the Bible and all religious and philosophical texts did the same. Thus, these profoundly intricate documents were born. Peterson continues:

> *The Bible is, for better or worse, the foundational document of Western civilization (of Western values, Western morality and Western conceptions of good and evil). It is the product of processes that remain fundamentally beyond our comprehension.*

The Bible is a library composed of many books each written and edited by many people. It is a truly emergent document—a selected, sequenced and finally coherent story written by no one and everyone over many thousands of years. The Bible has been thrown up out of the deep by the collective human imagination which is itself a product of the unimaginable forces operating over unfathomable spans of time. Careful, respectful study can reveal things to us about what we believe and how we do and should act that can be discovered in almost no other manner.

Studying history provides us with a glimpse into the developments of any vast civilization, the rich and the poor, the greatest war heroes, and the most influential philosophers. But our world is not the world it once was. Our world has changed more in the last hundred years than it has through all of time since its theoretical creation in the book of Genesis, where God molded our modern world as if from a mound of clay. According to Genesis, God created the oceans and land, the majestic birds of the sky, the proud beasts of the plains. God created towering mountains, although humans built civilizations to stand atop them.

Rule over the fish in the sea and the birds in the sky and over every living creature that moves on the ground. (Genesis 1:29)[51]

Man wrote of God creating the sun and the moon:

265   *Arrows of Youth*

God made two great lights—the greater light to govern the day and the lesser light to govern the night. (Genesis 1:16)

I like the simplicity of this line. Imagine walking on the moon—the particles of dust beneath one's boots, the vacuum of silence, and the incomprehensible depths of blackness. I look into the dark rainy sky and I don't feel alone. I know where I am, and I'm not the only one who feels the rain. But being in outer space and standing on the moon, staring into a blackness deeper than Earth's core—how can we believe our planet is the only one of its kind?

In the sixteenth century, Polish mathematician and astronomer Nicolaus Copernicus explained our planet's revolution around the ball of fire that is the sun,[52] *the greater light to govern the day.* In the twentieth century, Albert Einstein devised a theory to explain the stars and the blackness, signifying that perhaps what's in our minds is as complex as what's out there.[53] We've found the answers for how we came to be. But our day-to-day existence—the trivialities of the mind, the senselessness of love and passion, and what separates good from evil—remains a quest of discovery on which each individual must embark to find their own answers.

The New Testament, written after the death of Jesus, is a culmination of teachings written by the pen, and driven by the human mind. Like still water gathered in a shallow well, a reflection of those who look in it, the Bible is ambiguous and will show one a version of their own reality. In the pre-modern world, God often provided the greatest sense of meaning.

I wonder if it brought inner peace to stare at the moon and believe it to be nothing more than a note in the symphony of the heavens. There's a comforting mysticism in not knowing what is, in believing in a heavenly realm that controls the nature of our simple world like some great puppeteer of the sky. When we believe fate's guiding the way, maybe it is. On a clear black night one may look into the sky and see the faint red dot of Mars, whose name comes from the Roman god of war.

The planet Mercury, named after the Roman messenger god, is known for its quick orbit around the sun. Neptune sits far out in space and watches over the blackness of intelligible matter, named after the Roman god of the sea. Our modern world is inextricably linked to the world of yesterday, to the world of two millennia ago, to 4.5 billion years ago. Maybe our reality isn't what we believe it to be; people just like us have crafted it, yet we assume these things are preordained.

Maybe God created nature and maybe he didn't—we think we have the answers, yet we can hardly understand ourselves. Reality is often as beautiful as the gift of sight. I look into the infinitude of the universe and know it's real; the sun and the moon are real, and the colors of a rainbow are real. But, are they? What is a color but a chemical reaction in my mind? Before my eyes lay the wonders of the temporal world. But reality on this rock can often be cruel; life is as fickle and evanescent as a shooting star, here and gone before we live it. With hardly any time, we have a choice: search for meaning ourselves, or trust the meaning of the past. Studying the Bible has shown me that the writing itself attempts to understand humans' relationship with the universe, and this relationship became known as God.

Arrows of Youth

THE IDEA OF GOD IS SUBJECTIVE. Humankind has given God meaning because God signifies what is beyond comprehension. We'll never be able to give a definite answer to the meaning of life, misery, or the passion of the heart. God, for so long, has been that answer. For many people, religion is the reason for living, a moral code to adhere to, and a reason to believe there's something beyond. Then they may live at peace on Earth. Before science answered many of life's inexplicable questions—the creation of the Earth and how humans came to be—religion provided the answer, for all things came to be through God, or the gods. Here, I'll focus on the Judeo-Christian God.

The Bible is a story comprising the Old Testament and the New Testament. The Old Testament tells of God's creation of the universe, how man and woman came to be, the human struggle against nature, mass exodus, and the rise and fall of kingdoms. If the New Testament describes how to live a life of love as an individual, the Old Testament tells how God sought to teach humans the danger in their ways. What we know of as history, the dawn of modern humans, begins in the Old Testament with Abraham, after the biblical flood.

> *Now the springs of the deep and the floodgates of the heavens had been closed, and the rain had stopped falling from the sky. The water receded steadily from the earth. At the end of the hundred and fifty days the water had gone down, and on the seventeenth day of the seventh month the ark came to rest on the mountains of Ararat. The waters continued to recede until the tenth month, and on the first day of the tenth month the tops of the mountains became visible. (Genesis 8:1-6)*

Arrows of Youth

What comes next I find to be beautiful yet incredibly complex in how it relates to our relationship with God, thus, ourselves. The passage continues:

> *After forty days Noah opened a window he had made in the ark and sent out a raven, and it kept flying back and forth until the water had dried up from the earth. Then he sent out a dove to see if the water had receded from the surface of the ground. But the dove could find nowhere to perch because there was water over all the surface of the earth; so it returned to Noah in the ark. He reached out his hand and took the dove and brought it back to himself in the ark. He waited seven more days and again sent out the dove from the ark. When the dove returned to him in the evening, there in its beak was a freshly plucked olive leaf! Then Noah knew that the water had receded from the earth. He waited seven more days and sent the dove out again, but this time it did not return to him.*
> *(Genesis 8:6-12)*

The dove and the olive branch signify peace between God and humankind. With so much history and unending conflict attached to religion, it's daunting to even open the Bible and attempt to understand its teachings. But when I read a passage like this, I consider how it isn't what's in the stories that turn us against one another; it's how humans have twisted their teachings because of our own damaged morality. Awareness, I've found, at least knowing what the book contains, brings a

sense of peace. Perhaps studying the Bible will provide something more
—*virtue.*

The Bible tells stories of redemption, how to treat others, how to find the light when the world appears bleak, and how to listen to oneself over the voice of the mob. The New Testament illustrates how to live a life of love beyond the self. In the first few millennia BC, civilizations were popping up simultaneously around the globe independent of one another. Fundamental inventions were giving life a different sort of meaning: writing, music, and new art styles were flourishing. Humankind was developing, and the more it did, the more people searched for the answers to our existence. The Bible is the story of human beings attempting to make sense of their time, just as we attempt to make sense of our own.

The Bible is a book of perspectives—of the authors who wrote the Old Testament in the first millennium BC and the disciples of Jesus who wrote the New Testament in the first century AD. Matthew, Mark, Luke, and John are key figures in the Bible, as their accounts make up the New Testament's history books. They each tell of the life and teachings of Jesus Christ in their own ways, ostensibly targeted at different audiences. It's debated amongst historians and interpreters of the Bible whether these men were there when Jesus performed his miracles. What's fascinating is how these different writers tell the same stories from different perspectives, and how they gained their information and sources.

Matthew, Mark, and Luke all tell of Jesus calling his first disciples at the Sea of Galilee. The way their stories differ in style shows that each had their own perspective of the scene. With the same facts, each story

Arrows of Youth

depicts something subtly different. The facts of history can often seem black and white; reading these stories together provides firsthand insight.

Matthew, Mark, and Luke aren't just names from the history books. They were people attempting to describe their modern day and the workings of Jesus, a man who enchanted the world with his gifts. Matthew was a tax collector whose original name was Levi. It's believed he was one of the original disciples of Jesus:

> As Jesus went on from there, he saw a man named Matthew sitting at the tax collector's booth. "Follow me," he told him, and Matthew got up and followed him. While Jesus was having dinner at Matthew's house, many tax collectors and sinners came and ate with him and his disciples. When the Pharisees saw this, they asked his disciples, "Why does your teacher eat with tax collectors and sinner?" On hearing this, Jesus said, "It is not the healthy who need a doctor, but the sick . . . For I have not come to call the righteous, but the sinners." (Matthew 9:9)

Matthew was ostensibly writing to the Jews to tell them that Jesus was the long-awaited Messiah as prophesied in the Old Testament, *the Hebrew Bible*. Matthew is considered the immediate connection between the Old Testament and the New Testament, as his writing provides the opening section of the New Testament. He clearly outlines his ambition to prove this connection by going down the list of Jesus' genealogy in the first chapter of his gospel. In Matthew, as well as Mark's

272

telling of Jesus calling his first disciples, the style is rather austere in how they depict Jesus calling these men to his side.

> *As Jesus was walking beside the Sea of Galilee, he saw two brothers, Simon called Peter and his brother Andrew. They were casting a net into the lake, for they were fishermen. "Come, follow me," Jesus said, "and I will send you out to fish for people." At once they left their nets and followed him. Going on from there, he saw two other brothers, James son of Zebedee and his brother John. They were in a boat with their father Zebedee, preparing their nets. Jesus called them, and immediately they left the boat and their father and followed him. (Matthew 4:18)*

It's believed that Mark wrote his gospel in the first century AD and was addressing the Roman people, resulting in a colloquial style of storytelling that aims at getting the point across without too much excess. Mark writes:

> *As Jesus walked beside the sea of Galilee, he saw Simon and his brother Andrew casting a net into the lake, for they were fishermen. "Come, follow me," Jesus said, "and I will send you out to fish for people."*

Arrows of Youth

At once they left their nets and followed him. When he had gone a little farther, he saw James son of Zebedee and his brother John in a boat, preparing their nets. Without delay he called them, and they left their father Zebedee in the boat with the hired men and followed him. (Mark 1:16)

The Bible is a form of art; the way Mark tells this story differs from how Matthew tells it, which varies from Luke's perspective. Luke was a doctor and the dear friend of the disciple Paul (Colossians 4:18), who likely wrote his gospel in the first century AD. He wasn't there with Jesus, as he states in his opening chapter:

Many have undertaken to draw up an account of the things that have been fulfilled among us, just as they were handed down to us by those who from the first were eyewitnesses and servants of the word. With this in mind, since I myself have carefully investigated everything from the beginning, I too decided to write an orderly account for you. (Luke 1:1)

However, like a doctor who scrupulously gathers all relevant information on a subject to put together a knowledgeable conclusion, Luke consults eyewitnesses and scrutinizes previous accounts to write his story. Luke tells the same story of Jesus calling the disciples from the Sea of Galilee, yet his story paints a different picture than Matthew's and Mark's. Whereas the other versions are to the point, I can vividly imagine the scene in Luke's telling. He writes:

One day as Jesus was standing by the Lake of Gennesaret, the people were crowding around him and listening to the word of God. He saw at the water's edge two boats, left there by the fishermen, who were washing their nets. He got into one of the boats, the one belonging to Simon, and asked him to put out a little from shore. Then he sat down and taught the people from the boat. When he had finished speaking, he said to Simon, "Put out into deep water, and let down the nets for a catch." Simon answered, "Master, we've worked hard all night and haven't caught anything. But because you say so, I will let down the nets." When they had done so, they caught such a large number of fish that their nets began to break. So they signaled their partners in the other boat to come and help them, and they came and filled both boats so full that they began to sink. When Simon Peter saw this, he fell at Jesus' knees and said, "Go away from me Lord; I am a sinful man!" (Luke 5:1)

I can feel the dusty air clinging to one's skin, the sharp taste of the lake on one's tongue, and the warm glow of the sun beating down on the fatigued fishers. Neither Mark nor Luke was there, yet they both tell a story that's ours to believe or reject. The images differ, but the details remain the same: Jesus was at the Sea of Galilee, which Luke calls the Lake of Gennesaret, where he attained his first disciples.

In the times of the Roman Empire, what must it have been like to craft the course of history with the stroke of a pen? These stories were the disciples' perspectives of the life and teachings of Jesus. They would take hundreds of years to spread and become accepted—but when they did, they changed the face of the planet as much, if not more, than the biblical flood.

As we have seen throughout history, the stroke of a pen can cause civilizations to rise and atrocities to occur. Nobody alive today was there at the time to hear Jesus preach, see him cure the sick, or watch him pray under the white light of the moon.

Perhaps the very men who wrote the Bible were dissociated from Jesus as well. Still, Matthew, Mark, Luke, and John found their life's purpose in spreading the gospel, the "good word." They dedicated their lives to something that they believed was bigger than them. Their cause was to spread the word that the son of God had died for our sins. But it isn't easy to grapple with how much religion has and continues to divide us. I believe God is whatever makes the individual live their best life while also improving the life of others. I agree with the following sentiment provided by Jordan Peterson in *12 Rules for Life*:

For Jung, whatever was at the top of an individual's moral hierarchy was, for all intents and purposes, that person's ultimate value, that person's God. It was what the person acted out. It was what the person believed most deeply. Something enacted is not a fact, or even a set of facts. Instead, it's a personality—or, more precisely, a choice between two opposing personalities.

It's dark when I pull into the sleepy town of Neskowin. Out of the bushes comes one, two, *twenty* deer, a herd bigger than I've ever seen, straight into the stream of my headlights. I jolt awake and slow down to watch them pass with my mouth agape. If God exists, then he, she, *it*—

the Source of all creation—is an artist. Every living organism, every facet of this world, is a brilliant piece of art. To perceive all of life and every day as beautiful is reason enough to believe there's something more than just existing.

We Mustn't Wait for One Last Fight

Inspired by Dylan Thomas's Do Not Go Gentle into That Good Night [54]

———

Thunderous words for
Mortal men,
Time slips away from
Hands like sand,

Where every passing
Day's a grain,
Confronting life with
Eyes and pen.

No plan to wonder
Should have been,
When we're embraced
By that good night,

Do what you must to
Make it right,
Exist through fire, loving might,
We mustn't wait for
One last fight.

The heavens speak when our
Time's near,
Until then there's no

Well laid map,
Though that's not something
We must fear;

Rather embrace uncertainty,
Honor the breath
Which we hold dear.

What road procures our
Heartfelt aims,
For there's not one path
To the night,

Still feel the sun,
Its roaring flames,
Its gentle glow
Casts morning light.

Live life now, don't wait to be,
When darkness comes,
The moon still shines,
So too the stars, spiritual guide,
Rejoice in light, a soul that's free.

22

ANCIENT GHOSTS & MODERN HEROES

THE STRENGTHENING STORM NEVER LETS UP. I arrive at my Airbnb in the evening, mentally exhausted from the inclement coastal drive. With several bags hoisted over my shoulder, I fumble with the abnormally sized key to get it in the door. It creaks open. When I step inside I laugh after setting down the bags. The room is intensely nautical-themed. Colorful glass balls hang from the ceiling above a wall-to-wall window that looks out at the beach. Picture frames with whaling decals line the walls; there's a rack of about fifty VHS movies, all classics that I have no intention of watching, next to a small, chunky television.

Other knickknacks fill the room, those found in a neglected sailboat that has sat in the harbor for a few too many years. The kitchen is bare, save for a tin teakettle with flowers painted on it. There's a musty rocking chair in the room's corner by the large window. I'm close to the beach, yet can only hear the crashing waves and the falling rain; it's too dark to make out any details of the landscape. I start a boil for some tea and pour a glass of whisky into my tin camp mug to warm my spirit. After the long drive, the burning liquid tastes sweet and relaxing. I feel the raw energy of the sea emanating from each crashing wave as I give the rocking chair a try.

The beach seems different from Washington. In Olympic, the beaches serve as resting grounds for sleeping giants. They're serene amongst the chaos; everything seems to work in harmony. Neskowin is what the world looks like when the giants wake. The chaos is more erratic and uncontrolled. I hear the distant squawking of birds muted by the swashing water. The wind howls and carries the rain across the sky in a perpetual gust.

When I told people I was going to Neskowin, most couldn't confidently place it on a map. Hell, I didn't know it existed before this trip. Still, it roars, and I'm content listening to the sounds of eternal growth and decay. If I close my eyes, I can imagine being in a forgotten lighthouse stowed away on the coast of Scotland. I imagine the sounds I would hear—the sea, the birds, the wind, and the rain. That's what I hear. The world is biting; it never ceases to display its strength. I open *The World Is My Home* and am comforted by Michener's tales of adventure.

He spent a lot of time in Scotland's Hebrides, an archipelago off the country's rural west coast. Reading about his Scottish sojourn transports me to a time and place different from anything I've ever known, but similar in energy to what I'm experiencing now. Michener spent his life obsessed with the unique destinations that enrich our planet. But what kept him continually engaged with the world was meeting the fascinating people who bring it to life. In the Hebrides, he stayed in a stone cottage with an elderly woman reminiscent of a time long ago.

As I read his story I ask myself, *Could I live that type of life?* Moving from country to country, picking up and readjusting, uncomfortable, unsure, often alone. I know I could. I'm not ready to settle. There's so much out there—*this is the time to get lost*. We can only learn so much about the world by staying comfortable, surrounded by what we know. When we're put into uncomfortable situations, growth begins. Our mind shifts as we realize the way we do things isn't the only way. Our biology adapts to new and challenging situations. That is what I crave.

When we're put into the unknown, we ask ourselves the difficult questions: *How can I use this discomfort to grow into all that I'm meant to be?* The unknown is the opportunity to come to terms with who we truly are. When we're out there and alone, our mind, our inner voice and our body are all we have. We must learn to love that person, the sum of each entity of self. We better *at least* get to know them.

THE MORNING SKY IS BLUSTERY AND DIM, as if I'm still asleep. It's 7:00 a.m. I turn on the lamp next to the rocking chair. It fills the space with a warm orange glow. I had an unpleasant dream that recurs more often than I'd like. Like my dream in Forks, this one eerily resembled reality, yet was oddly different. I'm running from some terrorist plot. Shooters are attacking my undisclosed location. I escape through back streets, hopping fences and taking abnormal routes atop buildings. *Why am I always running in my dreams?* It's exhausting. When I wake up I feel like I've been running. My heart pounds, my legs are shaky, I don't know what to think.

I sit on the side of the bed covered in a thin layer of sweat from the heavy blanket. What am I running from? I often think about what I would do if that were an actual situation. If I was in a public train or a square and heard a gunshot, would I run or try to help? What does it mean to be truly courageous? Perhaps it takes bravery to break from the social constructs of our day, to be a leader and step up for something bigger than any individual, although universal. To be brave, perhaps, is to bring to light the demons which we all face, yet seldom confront, at least in the exterior world.

The contemporary Norwegian author Karl Ove Knausgaard inspired me to become a writer with his *My Struggle* series. Knausgaard is just a man, yet being human can be remarkably heavy. It takes bravery to be completely vulnerable, but showing the world who we are and what we're confronting does more than ease the societal pressure on our individual shoulders. It connects us, binds us, and relates our universal human experience in a way that says *It's okay to hurt. It's okay to be afraid. It's okay to be you. Because I'm just me; let's be us, two individuals, together.* Knausgaard writes in *Book Six:*[55]

> *There is something all of us experience which is the same for all human beings, but which nevertheless is seldom conveyed apart from in the private sphere. All of us encounter difficulties at some point in our lives . . . These things are not represented and seem not to exist, or else to exist only as a burden that each of us must bear on our own.*

Through his writing, Knausgaard hopes to grasp his father's death. The story becomes his interpretation of his past and what it means to be a soul searching for meaning, love, connection, and a way out of the pain. We go about our seemingly trivial lives, yet the simple pursuit of becoming an increasingly better individual is a heroic story of adventure, irrespective of who we are or where we come from. It's unmanageable to get out of bed when we don't have any reason for living. When life becomes bereft of meaning, we fall deeper into the void of irrelevancy and lose sight of the fact that getting up, giving our best and striving to be at least incrementally better is a surer path to glory than conquering all the lands of antiquity.

The way out of misery isn't through the striving of perfection. The road to perfection may manifest itself in unjust ways, such as feeling the need for more in the exterior world, or placing unnecessary burdens on ourselves. It's through realizing our individual lives do matter; not merely for our own sake, but for the sake of all those whom we will ever influence. In caring for ourselves and at least giving a damn by aiming at some greater ideal, we sow seeds of goodness. Through striving to get better, being kinder to ourselves, and seeking something deeper that we may never understand, we find our reason for living.

Throughout history, something like purpose, tyrannical as it is, came to kings and rulers because they felt more powerful with each city and town that succumbed to their wrath. Our soul desires expansion, which is often manifested in the physical world. As the soul expands, so does the individual's need to attach to things: a title, a name or status. But our title won't come with us when we leave this Earth. All that will remain will be the lives we've touched through our own imperfect striving to become a better, *not a perfect,* person.

At the turn of the nineteenth century, Napoleon Bonaparte strove to secure power to ensure his name lived on through time immemorial. In our present day, fame means something different from what it did a couple of hundred years ago. At its foundation, however, it's the same. We want to feel relevant, at least in our own eyes.

Like any human, the legendary Russian author Leo Tolstoy had his faults. He battled earthly demons; his soul's expansion in the physical realm drove him to the brink of despair. He didn't travel there alone. Still, Tolstoy represents a man who lived with his whole heart and soul while on this Earth. When he left, there was nothing else to give.

A book, a timeless book, asks the reader to see through the author's eyes, hear with their ears, and feel with their heart. I traveled through history when I read Tolstoy's *War and Peace,*[56] one of my favorite books depicting the tribulations of Russian life during the Napoleonic Wars. Napoleon's campaigns took place from 1803 to 1815 due in large part to the power vacuum left in the wake of the French Revolution. As I read *War and Peace,* I existed in the Russian palaces and on the battlefield illustrated on the page.

I became an observer of an unfathomable time and place. As I read —*watched*—the scene unfold like some omnipresent phantom, the inner battles undergone by each character magnified the depths of my soul. With any life-changing book, I play the role in my own reality. *I question my morality.* In doing so I strive to become a better man. That's all a book can ask of a reader.

Stefan Zweig's autobiographical *The World of Yesterday*[57] tells the story of Zweig's life at the turn of the twentieth century and throughout the two Earth-shattering world wars. It provides a fascinating account of the pre-WWI years in Europe, a time of false security and the shifting tides of imperialism. Zweig describes visiting Leo Tolstoy's grave at Yasnaya Polyana, the Russian estate where Tolstoy grew up. Zweig writes:

> *Away from the road and lonely, this noble shrine lies shaded in the forest. Guarded by none and watched by none, merely shaded by a few big trees. These towering trees, Leo Tolstoy planted himself. His brother Nicolai and he as boys had once heard from some village crone a proverb, that happiness would prevail where trees were planted. Nameless, the great man lies buried, no cross, no tombstone, no inscription.*

Tolstoy's grave is beautiful in its simplicity. Nestled in the forest, his spirit, damaged as it may have been, lives on. *War and Peace* portrays the essence of life's magnitude, its delicacy, its spirit, and its pain. One of the most powerful scenes in all of fiction embodies what Tolstoy's life stood for, the ancient tension that takes place within and in the temporal; the expansion of the soul, whether for good or evil.

Amid the throes of battle, the French army takes prisoner the Russian Prince Andrei. Emperor Napoleon, a man who razed country after country to secure his place in history, approaches the prisoners. Even though they're fighting against one another, Napoleon is Prince Andrei's hero. He's the most famous man in the world, a deity even in the eyes of his enemies. With his last breaths slipping away, Prince Andrei is mystified as he looks into the eyes of Napoleon. Tolstoy writes:

> *Now, with his eyes fixed directly on Napoleon, Prince Andrei was silent. To him at that moment, all the interests that occupied Napoleon seemed so insignificant. His hero himself seemed so petty to him, with his petty vanity and joy in victory, compared with that lofty, just and kindly sky.*

Behind Napoleon, Prince Andrei gazes into the ethereal, clear sky. Nothing is more powerful, not even Napoleon himself. He realizes Napoleon is just a man. Nothing of war, the day-to-day worries, or the pursuit of power which Napoleon goes to the end of the Earth to secure, mean anything to Prince Andrei anymore.

> *Prince Andrei thought about the insignificance of grandeur, about the insignificance of life, the meaning of which no one could understand, and about the still greater insignificance of death, the meaning of which no one among the living could understand or explain . . .*

How, Prince Andrei wonders, is anything that we desire—fame, relevance, prestige—as worthwhile as a moment to stare into the vastness of the clear blue sky? The scene continues:

Nothing, nothing is certain, except the insignificance of every-thing I can comprehend, and the grandeur of something incom-prehensible but most important!

We comprehend the material world and believe that's where value derives, causing us to perpetually chase the illusion. Yet, we can't understand what's within us, nor can we fathom the grandeur of a clear blue sky, the spirit, or the heavens. We struggle to explain what goodness truly is or the complexities of love. Yet, as Tolstoy writes, these things are most important of all. A life dedicated to the incomprehensible search for meaning is a life well-lived.

We think importance comes from the big things we do, but it doesn't. Our public, monumental moments of competence don't define us. We're lucky if we even have any. If we do, we should be proud; but then what happens? When we're alone in our thoughts, in our depths of self, in the throes of despair, who are we then? Are we a figment of the imagination if nobody's there to witness our good deeds? No—our fearless actions to stand up, get out of bed every day, and continue striving for some ideal that only we can understand make us all too real.

How we live when nobody is watching makes us who we are. What we do every day gets us closer or further from that ideal. How do we carry ourselves? Are we light and joyful, laughing as much as possible even when there's nobody to hear? Do we live with intention and care for others? These are the characteristics that matter, not for anybody else, but for ourselves.

Perhaps living to spread our light is the modern work of a genuine hero whose soul is grander than all the lands Napoleon sought to conquer. To be a modern hero may be as simple as keeping a smile on our faces. I'm here to learn to love who I am, with all my faults and imperfections. We all deserve love, but to love others we must love ourselves. *Hurt people hurt people.* Those who move through life with grace and seek to bring others up recognize the imperfections as part of the game. To strive for perfection leads to destruction. To thrive in love, unconditional love, that's human, and more divine than any false idea of perfection. To lighten the burden that another human soul feels, *that we all feel,* as Knausgaard says, just by giving your best, that's the work of a modern hero.

I HOLD MY HAND BENEATH the rafters outside the window and catch the drops of rain showering down on the wooden deck. I gaze upon Proposal Rock just off the shore. It's still difficult to make out in the dark blue light of the stormy dawn. Swathes of rain fill the sky, carried by the wind. The water of the Pacific Ocean moves every which way.

The sounds kept me stirring all night; the waves, the wind, the creaking of the door to the deck when the wind blows it ajar. The cool air would drift into the room and lull me back to sleep, into the dream state once more. Light pervades the room as the morning progresses. I fill the teakettle with water and turn on the stove to begin the boil. The color of the ominous rock is becoming noticeable—dark green, and black as an abyss. I can sit and listen to the sounds forever, deeply immersed in my hero's journey, past the point of no return.

Light has peeked through the clouds, beckoning me to get out there and join in on the fun. I put on my jacket, head out into the storm, and walk about fifteen minutes down the highway to find a route to the beach. My body feels good as I stretch my legs in the noontime rain.

After eventually finding a path through a beachside community, I walk back and forth along the damp brown sand, breathing deep and taking in the salty sea air. Houses line the beach; who lives in Neskowin, Oregon, I wonder? I warm up quickly as the now bright light shines down on me and warms my skin. I take a moment to sit on a rock and stare out into the waves. Light continues to fight its way through the clouds, and it's turning into a glorious winter's day. Further down the beach, there's a river that runs past the cottages and funnels into the ocean.

I walk down to observe the river and kick around while waiting for nothing in particular. I watch how the water moves over the sand mounds in the river and creates stationary waves; they don't go anywhere, they just roll in place. A small crab floats downstream on its back with its legs up in the air; I wonder where it will lead and what it's thinking, if anything at all. I imagine what it would be like to be the crab floating down the river into the ocean. It's so small compared to me, and I'm tiny compared to the behemoth Proposal Rock, which the crab is heading straight towards. What is a rock of that size to a crab? Bigger than a skyscraper? More massive than a mountain? What is a river, an ocean that constantly flows? Perhaps it's oblivious, as a life of digging aimlessly through wet sand is all it's ever known.

Is the crab any happier with its relative fate and its relative existence? We as human beings expect more in life and feel inept when we don't achieve greatness. We feel inadequate when we don't live up to our potential. But the crab only knows sand, endless amounts of sand. It's like a monk who has simplified life to nothing but breathing and cleaning. If that's all you know, are you happy when you have it?

Now, like the human soul floating from Earth to the afterlife, whatever that may be, this is the crab's moment to stop digging for a while. Proposal Rock might as well have been Mount Olympus to the crab on his way to a new beginning on a very stormy day in Neskowin, Oregon. This could be the ride of its life, the river of purgatory on the way to heaven or hell. I don't know the character of the crab, so I can't say for certain.

A storm cloud arrives from the distant end of the beach and in a matter of ten to fifteen minutes, it's pouring rain where it was warm and glowing just before. Being in Neskowin is to experience the scenery completely change in the blink of an eye. I'm not here to conquer a new hike. I'm here to stand on the beach as the day turns from a dark, tumultuous dawn into a golden afternoon. The second storm has come. I feel the shift in energy. Everything becomes white. I wrap my camera in a ziplock poncho—the cheapest travel accessories come in most handy.

The tide goes out and I notice what actually brought me to Neskowin. The remains of the ancient spruce trees known as the Neskowin Ghost Forest protrude from the sand. I had only an idea of where these petrified trees were located. This beach is the spot. Yet when I arrived, they were nowhere to be seen. I scanned the surf, looking for any sign of them. Then they faded from my mind. But as the rain has pounded down and the tide has pulled to the horizon, the trees have emerged like the remains of a ghostly shipwreck in the shallow surf.

As the tide flows out, I run into the waves to observe these strange remains. They're interspersed along the beach in an eerie formation, from the cove at the far side of the shore to Proposal Rock. One emerges here, then one there, like a compilation of individual stars that together create the constellation of a long-forgotten forest. The rain is pelting down at this point. Yet in another thirty minutes the weather changes once again. The sky fades from the stormy, almost blinding white rain into a dark and dry evening. When I'm back in the room it feels as though I've returned to my Scottish lighthouse.

In Portland, a friend told me that after Olympic National Park, the beaches in Oregon wouldn't compare. I thought to myself, *Every place is beautiful for a reason.* I knew it wouldn't be the same experience. But I also knew it would be beautiful. It was, in its own ghostly way. In the room I lay on the hard floor listening to the sound of the ocean and the rain, a dog's bark, a faint call, the sounds of existence—they become peaceful white noise.

Arrows of Youth

NESKOWIN

GHOST FOREST

Feel the Rain Fall from the Sky

Feel the rain, leave the umbrella
Embrace the teardrops from the sky,
Feel the smile form on your face
Look above when asking why.

Tears of pain and tears of joy,
Feel the tears fall from your eye,
A rush of overwhelming joy,
An answer comes to questions why.

Not a word and not a reason,
Spoken language of the season;
Feel the rain fall from the sky,
Look above, and you'll know why.

23

THE LIGHTHOUSE

BACK ON THE ROAD, I LEAVE NESKOWIN AND HEAD towards Fort Bragg in Northern California. I'll be staying with Thatcher, one of my closest friends, before heading to San Francisco. Thatcher bought his first house in the former lumber town of Fort Bragg, which lies a few hours north of San Francisco. The job is a buy, gut, live, and flip. I have to see how it compares to our former college house in San Luis Obispo.

The Barn, as it came to be known, had passed through the generations in Thatcher's family, from the oldest brother to middle, then to Thatcher and our gang. I don't know how I've been so lucky. Thatcher's family became all of ours, as his parents would often come down to fix or improve something, like installing a new fridge on an unassuming weekend. Thatcher's dad, Reed, is akin to Jesus in my eyes. As a carpenter, the guy can walk on water, fix anything, install a barn in the backyard (hence the name) or create a fireplace out of a few rogue bricks. If we had a problem, he'd fix it with a smile; then we'd all share a beer or two after a day of solid work. Thatcher has taken up his radiant heart and caring demeanor.

The rain is coming down like the cascading arrows of an ancient army. It's the perfect day to listen to an episode of *Dan Carlin's Hardcore History*,[58] which are typically four- to six-hour podcasts that dive deeply into history's lesser-known stories. Knowledge and learning are fluid concepts. We can study facts for a test until our brain feels shriveled and throbs, but the facts often fade from our memory when that test is over. What's the point of learning, then? After I graduated from college, I became obsessed with learning because I was no longer doing it for a passing grade. I began learning to quench my thirst to know about the world. I realized how, in whatever moment of life I'm in, the quest for knowledge alters my mindset to see the world around me from a new perspective. To me, this is the genuine spirit of learning.

Dan Carlin unpacks the dense story of Julius Caesar battling the Celtic Gauls in his Gallic campaign of the 50s BC. Carlin's podcast is unlike any other because of his honest enthusiasm for each concept he explores and the sheer detail he provides. His voice is raspy and low, yet clear and wonderfully engaging. The ceaseless rain provides the ideal stage for a pensive drive imbued with introspective thoughts and rich history.

When I listen to the story about Julius Caesar, I think about man's inexhaustible need for more. What drove Julius Caesar from the brinks of the known world into the forests of Gaul? First described by the Romans, Gaul was a region of Western Europe inhabited by Celtic tribes.

It encompassed present-day France, Luxembourg, Belgium, most of Switzerland, parts of Northern Italy, the Netherlands, and Germany, particularly the west bank of the Rhine.

What were the tribes that Caesar faced like in those ferocious battles? I don't need to remember everything I hear; my only grade is an answer to the question: *Did I enjoy thinking about the topic at hand?* I never took a philosophy class in school, and perhaps that was for the best. I found that philosophy often leaves a negative impression on students. We're asked to remember facts just for the sake of passing the exam at the end of the quarter. But one shouldn't study philosophy to remember the facts.

Philosophy (from the Greek *philosophia*) translates into the *love of wisdom*. Shouldn't we study philosophy, then, for the pure sake of enjoyment, to garner views unlike our own? If one loves wisdom, they seek all the different aspects which make life an enriching journey. I'm fascinated by historical figures such as Julius Caesar because I want to know, if possible, what went through his mind. I listen to Dan Carlin because I'm in search of wisdom. Wisdom doesn't just come from the painstaking study of facts, as our ancestors well knew. While studying history provides supplemental information to create a foundation to build upon, wisdom comes from moving, living, and observing how the actual world works with our own two eyes.

As I pass the nautical shops in the coastal towns of Lincoln City and Depoe Bay, I wonder how the tourist industry has stayed in business during the pandemic. Antiques, a ubiquitous burnt orange color like the Northwestern foliage, practically spill out of their front doors and turn to rust. There are Christmas lights draped along the roadside diners and antique shops, yet I can't help but pass them with a saddened heart. I imagine that these towns stand a dismal chance in our frayed economy. I consider how much of America comprises towns like these, coastal haunts that haven't changed in decades, just getting by, existing, and barely withstanding the stormy weather and dark days.

Their common resilience makes this country what it is—the barbecue joints and the clam chowder dive shops, the decaying country of yesterday making way for the country of tomorrow. This is America: the weird, the decaying, and the beautiful. It's time to make a change, but places like these will always be an intrinsic component of America's identity.

I'm lost in thought; the sound of rain has me in a trance; I hark to the stories of Caesar. When Carlin mentions Napoleon, Alexander the Great, and Julius Caesar, I can recall when they lived and what they did. I consider the motives of the triumvirate, which included Caesar, Crassus, and Pompey, who plotted to essentially conquer Rome. The facts will come and go, but for now they bring me joy. I drive along the coast and try to imagine the world in the first century BC. What was it really like? What did people look like? Like us? How could they? Yet, how could they not?

THIS IS PHILOSOPHY, the love of wisdom, not needing to be anything more than food for thought which brings me a day, a month or more likely a lifetime of joy. When we take a course and read only to enjoy a new subject, the knowledge seeps into our being under the surface. The effort we make to grow continually changes who we are, even if it's just in that month or two while we're taking a course or reading a book for fun.

I find gratitude observing the passing world with my own two eyes, lost in thought like thinkers of the past. The Greek philosophers found happiness in just wondering, an activity not needing anything more than space to breathe and time to do it. They studied the planet rather than merely existing in it. We may be breathing, our body may work, our eyes may function—but to foster a curious heart and soul which search for meaning and connection—that is to be alive. I listen to the stories as the rain increases in velocity. My windshield wipers are working as hard as they can; I'm in the midst of a serious storm.

These men and women that I hear about were, at their core, no different from us. They lived in a different time and a different place, but they too wondered: *What makes life worth living?* I think about the moment at the pandemic's onset when I met a man who changed my life, Alfred. Everything I've just mentioned derives from that fateful night. Through his passed down wisdom, he instilled in me a passion for learning that's attached to no grade, no test or degree. He showed me the value of learning for pure pleasure. Alfred undoubtedly redirected the course of my life.

On that early summer night, I left my mom's house in Malibu with no plan, only to clear my head. As the sun set behind the clean black silhouette of the mountains, the sky transformed into a shade of pink the color of a rose. It would rise somewhere far away and cast its light. As the sun disappeared, so did I into my thoughts.

At the end of the street sat Alfred, an older man who usually sits in his chair watching the sunset with neon green bracelets around his wrists so cars will see him. I've passed him before and shared a *good evening*, along with a few other cordial words. But that night, I felt like talking. I unconsciously sought some escape from the confusion in my mind surrounding the protests taking place. Maybe, he'd want to talk.

"Hey there," I called out, smiling and hopeful. "Unbelievable sunset, isn't it?"

"Not bad at all. And it changes every second." His comforting New York accent immediately brought me repose. It reminded me of my family. I stopped to consider his words. As the drop of light in the sky became more acute, the color grew more profound—from pink into a burning red. The colors flashed across the heavens until they became nothing. Blackness. Night.

"How long have you lived here?" I asked to spark a conversation.

"I lived in the neighborhood next door for seven years, and I've been here for three." A few others strode by and shared a quick chat, but I stayed. I had nowhere else to be.

"I'm Alfred." His voice was optimistic, his hair grey and lively and puffing out from under his cap. He was out there for a reason. This man had seen a full life and had decided to sit in the street and watch the sunset. Somehow, I felt like I should too.

"What do you do?" he asked with an affectionate rasp.

"Well," I thought about my answer with slight hesitation. "I'm a writer." We discussed my passion for writing, traveling, and reading. He told me his wife was a professor and that his existence had been primarily academic.

"Vincent, let me tell you, I'm not really of this world. I'm eighty-eight, and I know there were wars, I know presidents were elected, but I couldn't tell you much else of what's happened." I heard this and felt the connection between us. As a kid, before I became enraptured by history and philosophy, I felt connected to my grandparents merely through love; it didn't take more than that. This was the first time I felt an intellectual connection to anybody, especially a wise old man so full of life.

"Sometimes, Alfred, I feel the same way." I meant it. "Let me ask you: what's your favorite book?" The question took him aback.

"I could tell you were a smart kid! That is a question that reveals a lot about a person!" I smiled as I recognized the commonality between us. When one truly enjoys reading, it's an integral part of who they are. The love of reading is an essential part of my personality, and I had a feeling this would hit home.

He thought seriously for a few seconds, then confidently gave his reply.

"The Odyssey."

I stood in the street while Alfred sat. He was barely perceptible now except for his glowing green bracelets and amiable laughter. Our voices were the only sound in the air beside the gentle wind, discussing books and philosophy, topics that transcend time. I couldn't tell, but I needed this. It seemed he did too.

"Can I retract my statement?" he asked as if he hadn't stopped contemplating his answer since giving it. "If you want your writing to skyrocket, read Plato's *Republic*. That book laid the foundation for Western philosophy—it's the starting point for everything. As a writer, you don't just deal with words; you deal with ideas. That's where many ideas come from."

"I like that, Alfred," I replied, looking up into the darkening night.

"Write this down." I didn't have my phone or a pad and pen. "You should always carry something to capture your ideas. Ideas are like birds; if you don't shoot them, they'll escape." Of course, he had notecards in his pocket. He sprung up from his chair and took one out. He scribbled an online class to take on Plato's Republic through *The Great Courses.*

"Take the course, and you're going to have the most fun you've ever had this summer." He was happy for me, as if he had just revealed a secret that took him a lifetime to discover. He was sharing with me what brought him profound joy. Alfred provided me with an escape from reality into Classical Greece, an age where the inner workings of the cosmos were still a myth and our very planet held treasures yet to be uncovered. Today the world is too small to escape reality.

Maybe Alfred didn't know of the change taking place. Perhaps he didn't want to know, and I didn't have it in me to tell him that while we talked, looters were plundering Los Angeles like some ancient tribe. That's what it was like, tribal. The looting and destruction of the town I lived in broke my spirit. I didn't know how to handle it, how I could help or be a source of light. I didn't know I needed it, but Alfred gave me the strength to carry on.

Maybe watching the sunset every night provides him with faith in humanity. I long to be a part of that good, a piece of history not lost in the shadows but amongst the vanguard of light. Like the sun rising in the morning, there will always be a spark of light to overcome the darkness. Often, it must come from within ourselves. But other times, maybe when we need it the most, it comes from asking a simple question as a bridge between two souls: *What's your favorite book?*

I took the course on *Plato's Republic*, then an *Intro to Greek Philosophy*, which Alfred insisted on. I then took *The Birth of the Modern Mind*, a course revolving around the Scientific Revolution thinkers: René Descartes, Isaac Newton, Francis Bacon. When I listen to a lecture on Greek philosophy, I feel like I'm taking a walk around Athens with Plato and Aristotle, not learning to pass a test, but to understand what it means to be alive.

THE GREEK PHILOSOPHER ARISTOTLE contemplated and wrote about the difference between means goals and end goals, similar to the vehicle and destination goals that Jemal King discussed on the *Model Health Show*. Aristotle lived in the fourth century BC, during the golden age of Greek philosophy. In his *Nicomachean Ethics*,[59] he argues that all human action has some ultimate purpose. For example, in school, perhaps we view learning as tedious and anxiety-inducing because it's a means to an end. We study solely to pass a test. At least I did, and it didn't always work out. Yet, he argues, there must be some absolute purpose for living, some meaning to it all. If there were no end, then human action would be meaningless. We're always chasing, chasing, chasing—for what?

Aristotle argues that human life is not meaningless; he discusses what he calls the "highest good." This highest good, he states, is happiness (*eudaemonia* in Greek). We desire happiness for the sake of being happy; nothing more. But what is happiness, and why does it elude us the most when we believe it should be the most attainable? We buy new things to make us happy; we search for a new relationship to fill a void, assuming now, we will be satisfied. But we're not, and that's what hurts the most. Aristotle argues that happiness takes work within ourselves; it shouldn't take external goods.

He implies that a life spent primarily examining the world brings happiness. On my current adventure, I've found this to be true. Studying nature inspires us; it grounds and makes us realize what matters. What matters isn't what we're perpetually chasing—money, status, material things. It's what we already have—a mind to think, and space and time to do so, a connection with another soul, a repeating breath that rises and falls and sustains our thoughts until we are no more.

The way Alfred lit up when I asked him about his favorite book was achieving *eudaemonia*. Studying philosophy for Alfred is an end goal, not a means to an end. It filled him with joy, and nothing could provide more meaning. The same goes for the way he watches the sunset every night; he's in his eighties. To me, it seems others love him and he loves them. To me, it seems he's healthy. There's nothing else a man could want.

Aristotle was a student in Athens at Plato's Academy. Both Aristotle and Plato believed a life spent thinking critically is the most joyful life of all. Of course, these men were philosophers and loved nothing more than discussing the complexities of life. Naturally, they would say a life spent philosophizing is the most joyful life. I think Alfred would agree. Regardless of if we agree that philosophy equals the *most* eudaemonic life, we can take lessons away from their sentiments on what creates a good life. Aristotle was intensely interested in the study of nature with nothing more than the naked eye. This love of nature differentiated him from Plato. We consider Aristotle a theoretical philosopher, where theory comes from the Greek word *theoria,* meaning "looking at." He attempted to see the world as it really is.

He didn't have satellite images or telescopes; he examined the world and with his genuine curiosity, changed the way human beings thought about life for thousands of years. When I look into the dark and wintry sky and wonder what's truly taking place amongst the atoms and molecules, I forget, at least for a moment, about my worries. I'm captivated by the natural world, our home, with its beautiful colors and sights and smells, with its people I love and am lucky to call my friends and family, and that's not just my blood. To study the world makes life worth living; to learn for the pure sake of enjoyment is, perhaps, reaching an end—*eudaemonia.*

I SEE SIGNS FOR A LIGHTHOUSE as I make my way into the town of Newport, Oregon. The waves roll into the cliffside town and crash against the walls of slick black rock. The white lighthouse sits at the end of a rocky peninsula as a beacon in the tempestuous storm. I can't see much out at sea. The horizon is indistinguishable from the sky. The water is a dark grey, stressed only by the crests of white waves.

Lighthouses are commonly placed at the end of cliffs or hills in regions of the world where danger looms. They stand as beacons of hope, safety, and resilience. For a solitary sailor lost at sea amongst endless gales and rolling waves, a lighthouse means survival. The color is often white, signifying safety. A red lighthouse represents danger. The lighthouse serves as a beacon of stability in a chaotic world. I watch the Newport lighthouse take the brunt of the storm as I listen to a song that rocks me to my core: *The Shrine* by Fleet Foxes.[60] It fills me with inspiration, passion, and my own sense of resilience. The song starts with the gentle strumming of a guitar accompanied by folksy lyrics. The energy builds like the gathering of menacing clouds. Then, the chorus strikes like the first crack of thunder to let you know the storm has arrived:

Sunlight over me no matter what I do.

This line epitomizes what I feel in this moment, a wave of joy and light that nothing in the world can dim, no foreboding storm, no societal pressures, no fear, regret, or pain. I will embrace the storm because, through our trials, we summon the strength for growth. Through the uncertainty, the questioning and chaos, we discover what we're truly made of. I'm grateful for the storm.

I leave my car and find warmth emanating from my soul amid the falling rain and deadly sea. The water cleanses me down to my essence. I run up to the base of the lighthouse and gaze upwards towards its pinnacle; the shrine, a place of worship, a beacon of light. I'm here to learn about the world on this never-ending search for wisdom. *I'm happy.* I look up into the dark grey sky and beam. *Bring it on, whatever it is, bring it on.*

PART THREE
SUNLIGHT OVER ME

Spirit of the Hero

An image, reflected by the glass,
Days gone by have
Brought you here
Sundry in existence,
All that's present seems to pass;
A future self-alluring, thoughts
Which seldom seem to last,
Distorted by ascending smoke,
Hazy veil of fear.

Hand outstretched cuts right
Through illusions of the mind,
What's really there are hopes and
Dreams more real than reality;
You vanish into air, although
Seeking you may find
A dance of aether, clearing
Weather, warmth of sun
Entwined,
The rising grey keeps
Hearts at bay,

Though this is merely fallacy.
The smoke will fade and dissipate
The higher that you rise,
Image in the glass reflects
What's truly there;
A boundless spirit,
Covert in disguise,
The hero of your own life's story,
Beautiful and wise,
With vision cleared in
Empty space,
No longer fear to bear.

The smoke has cleared and
What you see;
The unknown is reality.
Empty, vast,
Not here nor in the past;
Dancing cells have come alive,
Ensure true aim—let go.
The spirit of the hero.

24
REALIZING MY DHARMA

NYIELDING AND TENACIOUS, THE STORM follows directly above me for the entire drive down the Oregon Coast and across the border into California. I call Thatcher and tell him I'm not going to make it tonight—the storm hasn't let up. I have to find a place to stop. I approach the town of Arcata and decide it will be best to spend the night and head to Fort Bragg in the morning. I call for a room at the Hotel Arcata inquiring about a respite from the rain. Arcata was first established in the late 1800s, which is apparent by the way the Union originally set up the town. A large plaza sits in the heart, the place where a political candidate might stand on an apple box a hundred years ago, beckoning the citizen's vote.

Homeless humans hunker down in practically every business entry-way; walking past them along the drenched sidewalk tears at my soul. Homelessness always has. Their rowdy conversations fill the restless air.

Arrows of Youth

I arrive at the hotel and open the thick glass doors into the lobby as if entering a saloon. The place is funky, but all I need is a roof. A Christmas tree stands tall in the discolored yellow lobby with fake presents surrounding its base; this makes me a little happier, but I'm out of it. The clerk looks terribly bored and gives me the room key, a real brass key. I lug my bags up the central T-shaped staircase. It's a scene where I can imagine a Western shootout taking place. I put the clunky key into the lock and turn to open the door. After the long day, I can't seem to do much other than tuck under the covers and slip away, listening to the rain in the plaza drown out the inebriated late-night conversations of Arcata. One conversation is too loud to be suppressed—a man explaining to a woman the proper way to skin a fish.

I step with my bag through the large doors and into the crisp morning. The town gleams from last night's rain. I walk around Arcata to stretch my legs before getting back in the car; a couple laps around the square should do. These are the kinds of towns I read about in *East of Eden*, which popped up during America's westward expansion. I'm fond of their simplicity—a central square with businesses surrounding it, a market, a hotel, a saloon.

All I have with me are the things I can fit into my car. After two and a half weeks on the road, I've found a sense of peace in that spareness. Changing our environment is a great way to free ourselves from the *things* in our lives that take up mental bandwidth. What we're left with is that which we carry with us at all times: our beliefs, our character, our heart. I leave Arcata and within an hour am winding through the Mendocino Forest, where light pierces through intermittent cracks in the trees. I'm thankful I didn't attempt the drive yesterday in the rain;

it would have been a nightmare. The forest glows in the afternoon sun; it seems like a fantasy. This moment is beautiful, for I don't have to do anything but exist in this forest of light.

I STOP TO FILL UP AT A GAS STATION just outside of the Mendocino Forest. There's nobody apart from a man working on a car in the auto shop connected to the decaying cherry red gas station that has several pumps. He notices me as I pull in.

"How can I help you, sir?" the man asks in a high-pitched, smoky voice. His eyes and facial features are sunk behind a pair of glasses, and he has long, brown, thin hair falling from under his black cap detailed with orange flames. His attention darts around like a frog. The green eyes behind his delicate reading glasses follow.

"Just a fill up, if you don't mind," I reply.

"Yup, sure thing." He opens the gas tank and begins fueling from the outdated pump. There's a charm to it. The scent of a gas station in the woods is one of those soul-nourishing, earthy smells one encounters on the road. I'm curious about this man's story.

"Are you from the area?" I'm unsure of where this question may lead.

"Oh, yup, yup, I live up in the woods just around there, been here a long time, yup, long time." His answer needs probing, so I ask a follow-up.

"This must be a fascinating place to live; any wildlife around here?"

"Sure is; we have bears and mountain lions up in the hills there," he points up into the hills on the other side of the highway. "Gotta watch out for the mountain lions. The bears won't hurt ya. They'll run if they don't have any cubs." His demeanor reminds me of a mountain lion, or maybe of somebody who rides a mountain lion bareback through these woods. Silence ensues.

"Yup, a guy came by yesterday and asked me to fix his tire. So I did. Gave me a hundred bucks!" He puts his hands a few inches apart as if he's holding the bill between his fingers and looks at it with gaping wide eyes. An explosion of shock charges his face.

"I was like WHAAAAAA!"

"There we go!" I hope he doesn't expect a Benjamin.

"There are good people out there, I'll tell ya."

I nod in agreement. "There are indeed, my friend."

I leave the gas station and feel a headache coming on. I don't know from what; I need water. My mom calls as I'm leaving the gas station. We haven't talked in a few days. I let it ring for a moment before I pick up the phone.

"Hey honey, how's it going?" It's good to hear her voice. Still, I find it hard to tell her much of what's been going on. I don't know why it's hard for me to say, "I have a headache and don't really feel like talking. Can I call you later?" I've tried to put off thinking about going home.

I can't find the words to tell her that this is what I want to do with my life. I want to be with nothing but my soul traveling the globe, learning about who we are as human beings. I want to take pictures of the natural world and the energy that wells up in the depths of ancient cities. I want to learn from other cultures unlike my own, garnering wisdom to help others get the best out of themselves. Mostly, I long to live a life creating something that matters; I want to tell her these things, but I can't find the words. Instead, I shut down.

"I'm good, Mom, just staying the course. No, I'm not dying to come home. I could keep doing this for a while, I think." She doesn't know what this adventure has meant to me. She wants me home, and I love her for that. But I don't know if I can break this exoskeleton while in the confines of what I know. Our shell develops when we're young to protect us from the world. I've outgrown my shell and I feel my being expanding. It needs a place to go.

"Okay, I'll call you when I get there. Love you too. Bye." When we hang up, I think about texting her or calling her back to explain why I was short. Why is communicating so often challenging? It's like I know what I should do to make myself better, but I can't get myself to enact it. It's all right. I hope she understands; maybe I want to feel like I'm alone out here. But life can get dark if we go at it entirely alone. Sorry, Mom. I don't really want to be alone. I know I never have to be.

THATCHER'S HOUSE IN FORT BRAGG is similar to our college abode, with the same quaint white picket fence and a wooden archway for an entrance. The temperature outside is frigid, but when I open the door, I am warmed all the way through my being.

"Reed! What a surprise, I didn't know you were going to be here!" My spirit immediately lifts when I see Reed; his goofy laugh, classic stories, and bull-like frame bring to mind our college days when we spent weeks with him building the backyard from scratch. As I said, the man can build anything.

He's exactly where I'd expect him—elbow deep in the fireplace. The living room is empty except for a fold-up table, and there's a bright overhead light coming from the kitchen. The place looks like an inviting work in progress, just as it should be.

"Hey, Vinny, how you doin'?" He slowly ducks out of the fireplace and turns to see me. The layer of dust and chalk marks on his shirt and pants give him the look of a seasoned carpenter worth his salt. Reed casually stands and gives me a fist bump.

"I am fantastic."

I look around, and don't see Thatcher.

"Your trip sounds incredible! We heard it's been pretty stormy throughout Northern California and up there in Oregon."

"It has been the trip of my life." I mean it more than anybody can understand. "I've loved the rain; Olympic National Park is like nowhere I've ever been. In the morning, snow covered the ground and then in twenty minutes I could be at an absolutely wild beach or an icy rainforest."

"Oh, you're a real naturalist then, if you like the rain." This is the highest honor Reed could give me; a man who spent his youth working on salmon ships and embarks on a snow camping trip every year to build igloos in the mountains. If loving the rain means I'm a naturalist, then sign me up.

After chatting, I venture on my tour of the house. In the bedroom by the front of the house, I find Thatcher in front of a large experimental microscope. The room's empty, save for Thatcher, the microscope, and a blow-up bed. I burst out laughing at the sight of a butterfly wing on the screen facing me, magnified somewhere, I imagine, between a hundred and a thousand times. At this range, it looks like the beautifully intricate scales of a dragon.

Thatcher is sitting on a small stool, deep in thought with his face several inches from the screen. The locks of his black hair swing in front of his face as he studies the butterfly wing. He finishes what he's on and pops up, all six-four of his frame draped in a fur coat to stave off the cold. He gives me a big bear hug—Papa's home. After finishing up his work, Thatcher brings me out back to the massive wooden barn.

"Anywhere you ever live, there has to be a barn!" I say as he opens the door to the commodious space. An evening light permeates through the high-ceilinged window. Thatcher lived in the barn at our college house. It was his domain, his beat lab. We grab a couple of bikes and set out for an evening ride along the rolling coastal pathways. We cruise over railroad tracks, through the wavy brown seaside hills sandwiched by the ocean to the west and the remnants of old lumberyards to the east. The turbulent ocean waves are beautiful at this late hour. I don't really know where I am, only somewhere where the land meets the Pacific, a single point on the California coast where the sky is aflame and the sun has nearly vanished.

"I want to show you something!" Thatcher calls from in front of me. We pull off at a spot that overlooks a small coastal inlet. We lay the bikes down and walk closer to the wild, dark blue Pacific. The sky is a burning orange and my face feels frozen in a smile. We walk up to a compass rose emblazoned on the concrete path at the ocean's edge—the west arrow points directly to the distant horizon.

"Check this out." He calls me over to a bronze plaque next to a bench looking out to the ocean. I lean in close to read the plaque.

"That is a lot to take in," I say, stepping back, looking into the horizon. The compass rose is to honor Fort Bragg's sister city of Otsuchi,

Japan, which lies on the same latitude line as Fort Bragg. Their overseas connection began in 2001, creating a bond where families and high school students could visit and live in the city opposite. In 2011, ten years after the program's inception, a tsunami in Japan rocked Otsuchi to its core. Some 12,000 of the 15,000 residents went missing, including Otsuchi Mayor Koki Kato, and Otsuchi Exchange President, Coordinator and Interpreter Katsutaro Yamazaki.[61]

I'm enamored by the relationship between these two arbitrary towns, but more so by the power of the scene and what it represents. Thatcher and I stand on the cliff's edge, taking in the moment together. Another world exists across this mysterious body of water. The sun acts as the great unifier where, no matter where we are in the world, we watch it fall and rise. On the other side of the world in towns like Otsuchi, the moon has descended; the day has begun. I savor being with Thatcher at the onset of life's next season—*post-school, post-covid*—there will always be another *post*. Once I finish school, I'll finally have my degree and be able to work. When Covid-19 ends, I'll get back to enjoying life. *After this journey, I'll understand my true purpose.*

During my time on the road, I've sought an answer from the falling rain, a sign, something like a *greenlight* that tells me what next steps to take. But perhaps there will never be an answer to the perennial questions of finding meaning, at least, not when we're desperately searching for it. As I drove through the peaceful trees of the Mendocino Forest, I listened to Jay Shetty's book, *Think Like a Monk.*[62] Something clicked, perhaps an answer to the questions in my heart.

Jay Shetty left his "typical" life in London after meeting a monk at eighteen years old. He saw that this man had genuine happiness, and felt there is more to life than the traditional path he was treading. After graduating from college, he put his career behind him to pursue the life of a monk. He realized that the happiness he sought wouldn't come from climbing the corporate ladder like his peers. He needed to do the spiritual work. After three years in the monastery, his mentor told him to leave and share what he had learned with the world. I'm thankful that he did. Shetty explains that the ancient Sanskrit word Dharma roughly translates to your calling. He says in the book:

> *I see Dharma as the combination of Varna and Seva. Think of Varna as passion and skills. Seva is understanding the world's needs and selflessly serving others. When your natural talents and passions, your Varna, connect with what the universe needs, Seva, and become your purpose, you are living in your Dharma. You can't be anything you want, but you can be everything you are.*

> *A monk is a traveler, but the journey is inward, bringing us ever closer to our most authentic, confident, powerful self. There is no need to embark on a quest to find your passion and purpose as if it's a treasure buried in some distant land waiting to be discovered. Your Dharma is already with you. It's always been with you. It's woven into your being. If we keep our minds open and curious, our Dharmas announce themselves. Even so it can take years of exploration to uncover our Dharma.*

When I heard this, I thought about the reason I came on this trip. It's to find my *Dharma*. But as Shetty says, we don't *find* meaning; we are meaning. We don't need to *search* for love; we are love. We don't need to *be* anything; we only need to be. When life is so precious that a rogue wave can come and bury us at this very moment, what use is there in worrying? When our days are numbered and we don't know if a pandemic will rock our ostensibly mundane existence, what use is living in fear, anger, or regret?

To *be* is to wake up every day despite how we feel, utterly and completely grateful that the sun has risen once more. All we have to do is to be. Yet, there's a pressure to do more. That pressure comes from the exterior world, from what we assume is our path only because it's well-trodden. *The only path to tread is the one that takes us in.* When we're at peace within ourselves, we've established values—this is seeking our *Varna*. When our sense of self is in order, then we're at peace with the world and may tread lightly on this Earth. That's when we're ready to give something meaningful, something only we can give that says: *I want to help in any way I can.* That is *Seva*.

What surrounds us is the unknown. That's where we must go to find what we may give to the world. But perhaps there's an unknown waiting to be explored in each of us—mountains, rivers, and oceans of experience, just waiting for us to leap within. Going out into the world requires that we first go inward. To travel inward, as Shetty says, is a journey in itself.

There is no future and there is no past; there is only this moment. To live is to ask the questions of the universe; there's some greater plan for us all, but it's up to us to act. Perhaps the answers are in the questions themselves. Perhaps the answers are in the hearts of others, too; those that hurt, those that need our gifts, those that need a smile. What am I supposed to do with my life? *Live.* What if I don't love what I do? *Change.* How do I do that? *Take the next step, and then the next, and then the next, until you feel it in your heart that regardless of money, goals, and fame; regardless of the pain that will inevitably arise, you are full of undying love.*

I came on this trip to uncover my purpose. This is it. Watching this sunset with Thatcher at a point in our lives where sense seems to blow like a leaf in the wind is what I was born to do. To understand my *Dharma* takes more than merely thinking about myself. It takes being conscious of what the world needs, too. Right now, that's hope.

Freedom Lies Where Our Past Breaks

I feel the world within me.

Old-growth trees deeply
Rooted in the past,
They tell the story of the Earth,
Scars now seen are ones that last.

Beautiful, brown, intricate bark,
Like skin it's worn like armor;
Yet underneath that outer shell,
Reflective eyes portray the heart.

Heart of a tree that
Grows each day,
You look the same,
They'll want to say.
But they don't know the winds of
Change, that sway my branches,
Rearrange;
The path that once

I thought I knew,
That runs down deep
Where once I grew.

I grabbed ahold of Earth so tight,
Couldn't let go, took all my might,
To realize the strength it takes,
Yet freedom lies where our past
Breaks.

Like days outgrown
They've burnt to ash,
A lightning bolt comes
Like a flash,
So marvelous this force of light,
To wake up all that
Sleeps at night,
And burns away the past of me,
A bright new dawn,
I've come to see.

25

THE ART OF LIVING

M Y PERSPECTIVE IS AS FRESH AS THE RADIANT
morning sky. Thatcher and I are on our way to Albion, a small
town south of Fort Bragg and Mendocino where his family owns a
property passed down through the generations. We plan to get on the
Albion River and into the cove to drop some crab pots with Reed; three
friends, Thatcher, Reed, and me, enjoying one of life's simple pleasures.

I admire my friends' parents just as I do my own. Often, it's best to
sit back and observe. Last night, Thatcher and Reed went back and
forth telling stories. I listened, enjoying a glimpse into Thatcher's childhood. One story stayed with me. Thatcher was playing ping pong with
his older brother; for the first time, Thatcher beat him. His brother was
fuming. I've been in the same position as a younger brother; the taste of
victory over an older sibling is a moment of transcendence. Reed was
unaware of the result, and when he came outside and asked who won,

Thatcher's brother tackled Reed with the vigor of a raging bull. Reed acted out the scene and depicted himself lying face-up on the floor after being nailed.

"Wow," said Reed, "that kid's got spirit!" In this classic explanation, Reed communicated his life philosophy whether or not he knew it: *Every situation is what you make of it.* Reed chose to see the positive. He didn't ground his son for pile-driving him into the floor. Perhaps many parents would have asked: *What's wrong with this kid?*

It's our choice to see each moment negatively or positively; Reed chose and continues to choose the latter. He saw his son as spirited, not flawed. He laughed it off and showed his kids that he's on their team, their father first, but their friend, too. Parents must do what they can to keep their kids on the right path. But so much of being a kid is discovering who we are on our own. It has to be. But at that moment, Reed was also a friend—a friend tries to understand, no matter what. I admire the lesson imparted by Reed; whether he knew he was passing down a lesson or not, I took it as one.

THE ROLLING, GOLDEN FIELDS OF MENDOCINO County remind me of the hills of Tuscany, Italy, the land Leonardo da Vinci called home. I pass sheep grazing the bucolic landscape under the dazzling noon light. I feel a deep sense of connection with the Pacific Coast—*as this is my home.* The connection I share with this raw coastline will never degrade as long as I cultivate it. No place lacks beauty when we're able to lose ourselves in its subtlest simplicities. Home and memories are often interwoven, but from a perspective bereft of memories we find a different meaning, one where the most inconsequential experiences create the nostalgic moments to be remembered. This is one of those times.

I get a call from Thatcher. "Hey bud, follow me. I have to make a pit stop." We pull into the town of Mendocino and drive down a gravel road. I park behind Thatcher next to a graveyard that's withdrawn behind an arched stone wall. The roadside flowers of this idyllic town are vibrant and smell of fresh lavender—a peaceful place to lose oneself in the world within a blade of grass. Scents of fresh flowers and delicious food permeate through the gravel roads. The town constructs the buildings in an East Coast Maine style to portray a uniform fashion. We arrive at a pizza shack reminiscent of a hobbit home basking in the sun. It has a small, rustic backyard with an adjacent garden. A beautiful girl casually writes the menu items on a black chalkboard. She has a chic, comfortable style. This looks like a pleasant place to work.

People stand around and chat like it's an art show. A man in a fedora and a scarf picks up his pizza before us; I glimpse his pie and my mouth waters. The edges of the wood fire pizza are burnt with smoldering black pillows of char on the crust. The thick-cut pepperonis are sizzling in the center and the cheese is dark gold.

Thatcher picks up our pie; I stand back. I walk past the girl on our way out and my inner dialogue runs rampant—*Say something. Anything.* I try to make eye contact, but that won't do. *Say something!* goes the voice. I keep walking, one, two, three steps past, and I still don't do it. *When will you start speaking up?* I ask myself, or is it even me? We defy that voice in our head. Should we not? It tells us to do something we wouldn't normally, but often when it tells us to speak up, talk to a stranger, or stand up courageously for what we believe in, it's what we need to hear. Other times it does the opposite. We know we shouldn't listen to the voice: eat another slice of pizza, have another drink, or lash out in anger. Often it's in our best interest not to blurt out our thoughts. That's restraint, common sense—maturity.

But maybe there are times when we should heed the voice's call. The voice will lead us towards adventure and spontaneity if we acquiesce— but fear holds us back. Our inner voice is often senseless, but it's one thing that we'll never be fully rid of. A solitary trip, I've found, hasn't made it any quieter. That hasn't been the point. If our inner voice never leaves us, we must confront it and turn it into our greatest ally. It's no easy feat, but one worth tirelessly pursuing.

Stefan Zweig's biography of the sixteenth-century French Renaissance thinker Michel de Montaigne explores this relationship with the inner voice, something Montaigne valued practically over everything else.[63] Montaigne wrote:

> *The dialogue with the self is the highest level of art*
> *to be attained.*

Michel de Montaigne lived in 1500s France amidst one of the bloodiest conflicts in human history: the French Religious Wars. In the sixteenth century, being a Catholic or Protestant meant more than being a friend or neighbor. Caught in between this brutal age, Montaigne did something it seems nobody else could do: he sought beauty in humanity. Studying history makes one more acutely aware that human beings have endured unfathomable atrocities. Despite the world around him, Montaigne relentlessly sought what it means to be a human being who could not only endure such things, but find meaning in them.

What came was his *Essais,*[64] his individual works on life and death, inner thought, the joys of travel, friendship and communication. Above all, Montaigne sought to discover how to stay true to himself, *"rester soi-meme."* Montaigne's sole purpose was to master the art of living. He wrote his *Essais* as a spiritual guide to connect with his mind, body, and soul, not merely to endure the atrocities taking place, but also to live. He wrote:

> *My métier, my art, is to live.*

Montaigne has inspired me to pick up the pen and write through any adversity I face. Moreover, he's inspired me to *live*. His work laid the foundation for what we consider the modern essay, comprising 107 chapters of varying lengths and style, each with a specific theme. The word *essai* means to attempt or try, as putting thoughts on the page was, for Montaigne and myself, an adventure to embark on. The modern five-paragraph-essay infers one must know exactly what they will say at the onset of writing. However, it should be the opposite. After graduating from college and putting the dreaded five-paragraph-essay behind me, essay writing became one of my greatest joys. It allows me to try, at least, to understand myself and the world around me.

Montaigne wasn't writing to have his work published. Everything he penned was for him and him alone to understand what remained within his soul. Without uncovering what rests deep within us, the wind is free to send us drifting like a boat with no anchor, no spirit as a captain.

Montaigne dedicated himself to studying the depths of his own mind. He realized that life might exist all around us, but what we see, our reality, is determined from within.

This starts with the voice in our heads. It can feel as if there are opposing forces like the sun and the moon, battling one another for the sky's command. They ultimately seek harmony, as both are necessary to guide us through our days. Yet, the negative voice often has a way of overpowering the truth—the light, the authentic self. Many of us fear solitude because we're afraid of what's in our minds; without the time to truly dig deep, ask questions, and learn to honor our inner voice, we will never really be free. The fear of silence and the fear of boredom hold us down, but we must face that time alone. Montaigne writes:

> In the freedom of the arts, let us begin with the one which makes us free.

We have the ultimate authority to dictate that dialogue as we decide what thoughts to believe and which ideas to actualize. We choose to be courageous when we listen to our hearts and let them speak. Montaigne says:

> Communication is health; communication is truth; communication is happiness. To share is our duty; to conceal nothing; to pretend nothing; if we are ignorant to say so; if we love our friends to let them know it.

When religious wars ravaged all of Europe and turned neighbors against one another, Montaigne strove to find love in the world. To take

Montaigne's teachings and apply them to our modern day is to practice the supreme art of living: to know oneself. Montaigne writes:

> *Neither the position in the world, the privilege of blood nor talent makes for the nobility of man, but solely the degree to which he strives to preserve his personality and to live his own life.*

By the time Montaigne was thirty-seven, his life had essentially meant serving others. He had acted as a counselor of the Court des Aides of Périgeux and the Parlement in Bordeaux; he had served as a courtier to Charles IX, king of France. Then while away, he was elected Mayor of Bordeaux. Respected by both Catholic and Protestant nobility during the Religious Wars, they repeatedly made the request of him to act as a voice of reason. At that point, after giving so much of himself, Montaigne realized he didn't know what *himself* meant. He wasn't solely the man awarded the collar of the Order of Saint Michael, the honor he'd always dreamt of receiving. He wasn't just the mayor or the civil servant. He'd taken on these roles, and in doing so had lost touch with his essence, his identity—his sense of self. This is why he had to write.

During his time serving at the Bordeaux Parlement, Montaigne became close with the humanist poet Étienne de La Boétie. Étienne died in 1563. His death shook Montaigne. Without his dear friend to share his soul with, he began his *Essais* as a means of communication. The reader was now his friend. *The reader was him.* After his years of civil service, Montaigne launched himself on a quest to leave his home in Aquitaine, France and experience all Europe offered. He sought to unravel the truth of living through participation in society; he desired to explore the joys and struggles of the ordinary people he had served for so long. Zweig writes:

> *Out of the art of living comes the art of travel. Not a son and a citizen of any fixed place, but a citizen of the world, beyond any land or time.*

Montaigne inspires me to dance through life, not fearing the world unfamiliar to us. How, when cities burned and bodies littered the streets, did this man seek good in the world? How did he exist amongst such chaos? He did it through the only way he knew how—by writing, studying, and never settling for anything less than love for humankind. We are capable of despicable things. Yet we're also capable of forgiveness and connection. We don't have to live in a world that destroys itself like that of the past. We must study history to realize this.

I turn to Montaigne to see the best in people, irrespective of where they come from or who they are. I strive to see the best in myself, and I will make that inner voice my guiding light. Montaigne didn't suffer in vain. He penned one of the most extraordinary works of all time, different from a story of fiction, unlike a classical hero's journey such as *The Odyssey*. Yet, maybe they're not so different.

His *Essais* provided all subsequent ages with an insight into what it means to be a human being: the good, the bad, the beautiful, and the courageous. A hero of his own time, a hero of today, Montaigne used his pen to explicate the depths of his soul. In doing so, he's provided me and countless others with a means to better understand our own. I didn't speak up this time. I'm okay with that. There's always another opportunity to heed the call. But we must be willing.

I PASS OVER THE ALBION RIVER BRIDGE of Highway 1, the last wooden bridge on the legendary California route. Built in 1944, the narrow bridge is held up by long wooden stilts supported by a steel center truss. The bridge passes over the Albion River and the accompanying campground, where fishers and divers dock before heading out to sea or into the river. On one side of the bridge, the river opens up into a small ocean cove where we plan to drop the crab pots. The ocean water is a relatively calm, translucent blue. A mist lingers low in the air above the river mouth. It's a gorgeous day to drop pots. I follow Thatcher past a small grocery store and drive about half a mile down a dirt road before reaching his family's property. Reed is washing out the boat as we pull in, wearing worn-in rubber boots up to his knees, focused on nothing but the task at hand.

"Hey boys, can you help me lift this thing?" We get out of the car and put our shoulders underneath the back-end of the metal boat to empty the water. There are a few life jackets inside and two steel crab pots. A neon green butcher's knife and some frozen fish heads lay next to a bag of remains in the dirt. *Bait.*

"Vinny, can you cut off one or two of those salmon heads for bait?" Few tasks give a fisherman more pleasure than cutting the frozen head off of a musky fish. I'm glad to be given the honor.

"You got it." The knife is long and serrated and cuts through the frozen flesh with little effort. The eyes look at me like ghostly glass marbles.

"Remember, I have to be back around four for a Zoom meeting with Puerto Rico," says Thatcher from behind his Ray-Bans. The exuberance in Reed deflates like a balloon that's run out of helium.

"Okay, we'll make it." Reed gives the reassuring smile of a father. "But we gotta get moving."

"Roger that!" The bond between Reed and Thatcher is childlike and joyful, like that of two long-time friends. *Just be there for them, no matter what.* The parent's role is such an important one, but perhaps it takes doing less than we think necessary. Support your kid in whatever they aspire to. Impart your character through your actions. Set a foundation of rules and expect them to be followed, but allow room for growth. *Just be there.*

Perhaps this is most important of all: the need for somebody to tell us we are enough, we deserve to be held, we have more than only friends in our parents. Show them how to cultivate who they are; don't raise them to be who you are. A parent who believes in who we are is more powerful than anything.

When Thatcher's grandfather owned the land, he erected a Japanese Torii gate on the crest of the hill overlooking the Albion River. A Torii symbolizes a transition from the mundane to the sacred. This one is white and smaller than those exemplary red ones found in Japan at the entry points of Shinto shrines. Thatcher and I sit beneath its bent archway and eat a couple slices of pizza. We discuss life, family, and our shared love for all things Japan. *When you love your friends, let them know it,* says Montaigne. He lost the only thing that brought him joy in a joyless world—his best friend. We must never take our friends for granted. No matter what happens, we have each other to lean on. This life is an uphill road, one that's worth climbing together. Shoulder to shoulder under the Torii gate, we savor the unique landscape of Albion, where the river meets the sea.

WHEN REED IS READY, we attach the boat to the car's hitch and take off for the river. The plan is first to drop the pots in the cove and take a short cruise down the Albion River. Reed backs the boat into the serene green water lined on both sides with towering trees. When we depart upriver towards the open ocean, we pass several men standing on the dock with perhaps too much time on their hands.

A man in a cowboy hat and a dark blue hoodie sits in a fold-up beach chair with his golden retriever tied next to him. He raises a bottle of Budweiser in the air. Two others stand in idle conversation and turn to watch us as we go. Reed sits on the back of the boat with one hand on the handle of the four-stroke engine. He fixes his gaze on the horizon. Thatcher's in the middle, and I'm up front, all smiles. We pick up speed as we slice through the glassy water; the diffused waves roll into the river, causing the boat to rise and fall.

"Fuck, there are some waves!" yells Reed over the sound of the moving water. DSHH. DSHH. DSHHH. The boat takes each wave head-on and handles them well. I'm preparing for anything. We cross the threshold under the bridge and enter open water.

"It looks safe to drop off to the right!" Reed subtly turns the engine and the boat shifts in the slopping sea.

"Lean to the left!" commands Captain Reed. "Thatch, get the pots untangled and ready to drop!" I didn't realize how quickly this would all take place. This is a strike mission. Thatcher moves quickly and begins unraveling the bright blue rope like a kid who wants crab for Christmas dinner.

"Ready! Drop!" Thatcher and I grab the first pot by the sides of the metal cage and hurl it over the edge of the boat, quickly darting away to create tension in the line so it doesn't tangle.

"Alright, next one a little further out!" The warmth of the sun reflects off of the water and the spray of the waves kisses my face. The second pot goes down without a hitch. They'll stay out in the water for a couple of days before being retrieved, either with no dice or a boatload of delicious crab. A rogue wave tracks us down as we hightail it back to the river mouth. Reed stares it down. I notice something like fear in his countenance, but more like determination.

He cranks the engine's handle and we gun it through the shallow waves, outrunning the set wave like a gazelle defeating a hungry lion. We're back in the calm embrace of the river; our languid return begins. Those who saw us leave stand at the gates of Ithaca, *the Albion River dock,* awaiting the return of Odysseus and his men. Unlike Odysseus's men, however, we all return safely. We receive another Budweiser salute from the man and the dog. Mission successful.

The river snakes through the trees and becomes part of the surrounding land where seals bathe on the passing docks. They give us salty looks as we laugh at the enormous bodies of brown blubber.

On the hill's crest, we can see the Japanese Torii gate, *a transition from the mundane to the sacred.* We pass vacant houseboats in the middle of the river that look like something from *Mad Max.* I take over driving the boat as we head into a dam originally used to power a sawmill in the 1800s. Hawks fly by as if they know something we don't—a reason to be.

"I should probably get back pretty soon, Pops," says Thatcher before we cross the point of no return.

"Right, you drive." Reed gets up to let Thatcher have a crack at the four-stroke. The surface is perfectly still and reflects the pale blue sky, the soaring birds, and the shadows of the trees.

"WERE YOU GUYS DROPPING POTS?" A man with knee-high rubber boots similar to Reed's ambles over as we attach the boat to the back of the car. "You know you need a license for that, right?" he asks like it's his job to regulate. He walks slowly and has a dark red hoodie on with the sleeves rolled up to his elbows, as if his hands were grabbing lobster out of a tank. Reed turns from attaching the boat to the car by its rusting hook to face his accuser. First, he smiles.

"Yeah, we have them." Thatcher gives me an unforgettable look. He turns and flashes a subtle smile with his eyebrows downcast in question. He gives a slow nod to each side.

"This guy really thinks he can take my dad?" he leans in and whispers. I have to hold back my laughter. Reed gives off a relaxed demeanor by the way he faces the man. They square off. Reed comments on the dive shop logo on the hoodie and mentions a name—something like Marty McLeary or Dave Balemu—a name that, if mentioned, bears the weight of past legends and unrivaled diving experience. The man's shoulders soften, his eyes widen, and his chin lifts in respect. Thatcher and I lean back on the side of the car and listen.

They stand about eight feet apart and talk about the past: common connections, recent trips, successful drops, the different types of crabs, and the local dive shop haunts that are no longer around. There's no place I'd rather be than listening to the sounds of the birds and the tales of the sea.

Everything we do in life is a means to attain what Aristotle called the "highest good," happiness in itself. It's often the simplest habits and activities that provide that feeling. For a diver, there's nothing else to do but dive.

We think the key to life is more. But in reality, it's less—it's figuring out what makes us tick and doing it day in and day out. When we're able to find happiness through simplifying life, every day is part of the adventure. Reed has found this sense of peace in his own being. I feel it. Thatcher and I listen to the soothing stories before it's time for Thatcher to go. They walk off into the glare of the setting sun, father and son, friends. They are forever family to me.

The World Can't Take Our Joy Away

To rise each day the
Same old way,
And greet the teapot like a friend,
Flip through a book,
With time I may,
Write down the thoughts
I long to say,
My joy's innate, it knows no end.
The world can't draw what's
Stored inside,
Joy and happiness relate,
Though happiness
Requires a guide,
The right equation to abide,
Affected by the hand of fate.
But joy is different,
They can't take,
Never to lose, only to give,
Light from within that's
Hard to fake,

It shines the moment
When we wake,
What it truly means to live.
Throughout the day we'll
Meet our match,
From those who see life
Differently,
But joy's a fire, it may catch,
To heal a wound,
To sew a patch,
You never know who you'll
Set free.

Our happiness may come and go,
It's natural at times to be down,
We're human beings,
It's what we know,
But you're a king or queen,
A pro
So wear your joy like it's a crown.

26
CROSSING THE GOLDEN GATE

A FINAL STOP AWAITS: SAN FRANCISCO. I savor the California afternoon as I pass vineyards nestled in the hills on my way out of Albion. I come to a fork in the road. With no phone service, I can't tell which route will be faster. In one direction, I can continue on Highway 1 along the coast. The other will take me to the 101, which I assume would be quicker to the city. I ponder the heartfelt words of the poet Robert Frost:[65]

> *Two roads diverged in a yellow wood,*
> *And sorry I could not travel both*
> *And be one traveler, long I stood*
> *And looked down one as far as I could*
> *To where it bent in the undergrowth;*

Then took the other, as just as fair,
And having perhaps the better claim,
Because it was grassy and wanted wear;
Though as for that the passing there
Had worn them really about the same,

And both that morning equally lay
In leaves no step had trodden black.
Oh, I kept the first for another day!
Yet knowing how way leads on to way,
I doubted if I should ever come back.

I shall be telling this with a sigh
Somewhere ages and ages hence:
Two roads diverged in a wood, and I—
I took the one less traveled by,
And that has made all the difference.

I shall be telling this with a sigh, says Frost. I believe he means that looking back, if he took the easier path, the expedient route to happiness, he'd regret it. But he didn't. He took the road less traveled by—the route of greater resistance. I opt for Highway 1. It'll be a beautiful journey no matter how long it takes. I cross the bridge and embark on the path to San Francisco.

It's a foggy night when I cross the Golden Gate Bridge. The moon overhead is an arc of white light in the expansive night sky. After the past few weeks in the solitude of nature, I'm filled with energy as I cross

342

the great threshold into one of the world's most enchanting cities. From the surface of the moon, if I were looking down at the Earth, this bridge —a connector of two opposing land masses—would be negligible.

But down here, the Golden Gate Bridge exists; it's dark red, historic, and magnificent. The bridge provides human beings with the capacity to cross the mighty Pacific. But it's more than just a functional piece of infrastructure. It's a work of art, something that we created to provide meaning in the world. As I cross onto the bridge, I exist as a part of something truly essential, and not as a means to get from one side of the bay to the other. It's something essential to our existence—*beauty*.

I continue to peer up and let my gaze follow the cables higher into the night sky until they crescendo at the top of the towers. Often all that's visible above San Francisco's heavy fog are the tower peaks of the Golden Gate Bridge. Beauty serves as a pathway to heaven, the lights of the bridge like passing stars.

Why make it beautiful, like the color of falling autumn leaves, or the sky during the closing moments of dusk? Because beauty is ultimately what we seek as human beings. Jordan Peterson writes in his book *Beyond Order: 12 More Rules for Life*:[66]

> *We live by beauty. We cannot live without some connection to the divine—and beauty is divine—because in its absence life is too short, too dismal, and too tragic.*

We must be sharp and awake and prepared so that we can survive properly and orient the world properly and not destroy things, including ourselves—and beauty can help us appreciate the wonder of Being and motivate us to seek gratitude when we might otherwise be prone to destructive resentment.

We're inclined to seek beauty; as kids, we're destined to create a beautiful world. Yet as we grow up, we lose sight of what is beautiful. We ignore the beauty that surrounds us because we're focused on the trivialities of the day that ostensibly make us "mature," but consequently drain the innate divinity from our lives. We all have something within us to give to the world, yet we fear rejection before beauty can manifest itself. Peterson writes:

It is frightening to perceive the shells of ourselves that we have become. It is frightening to glimpse, even for a moment, the transcendent reality that exists beyond.

Because we don't know how to express the dormant potential within our souls, we settle. We stop searching for what ignites that spark in our being that only needs an inkling of recognition before it would light like a wildfire. There's beauty within each of us, something real and powerful, yet when it goes unused, we're prone to cynicism. We blame the world instead of asking ourselves where we may have faulted. We focus on the bleak reality of existence because our relationship with something transcending common sense has been demolished.

We don't have to settle. We recognize beauty in the world, even when we can't describe it. Beauty speaks to our souls; we long to create beauty and we seek it in ourselves. But we don't have to seek. The ability to recognize beauty in the world, perhaps before the words of others have disillusioned us, means there's something in each of us that's beautiful. Peterson writes:

> *Beauty leads you back to what you have lost. Beauty reminds you of what remains forever immune to cynicism. Beauty beckons in a manner that straightens your aim. Many things make life worth living: love, play, courage, gratitude, work, friendship, truth, grace, hope, virtue, and responsibility. But beauty is among the greatest of these.*

We've seen it in others. When another human being is absolutely consumed with what they're doing, we want what they have. Perhaps they've been encouraged. They've been told they have what's necessary to create something worthwhile. They haven't been stomped on by another hurt soul whose light has dimmed. Their energy is boundless and their smile awakens something in us that's been sleeping for too long. Peterson says in his Biblical Lecture II:[67]

> *That lifts your spirit up and gives you a little bit of hope, and maybe helps you continue on. That's obviously a call to being. It's a statement from your own soul that says, that's how you should be. Maybe, then, we get a chance to participate in what is good.*

The Golden Gate Bridge is good. Picking up a piece of trash on the beach is good. Not taking ourselves too seriously, the wonderful, incomprehensible, dazzling, imperfect beings that we are, is good. But we have to wake up. We have to realize every action affects the next one that we make, and that may affect somebody else, and so on. The world may try to tear us down. It will do everything it can to take our joy. But that doesn't mean it can. *It can't,* no matter what, no matter where, no matter why. It'll try to take our happiness, but joy is ours, and ours alone, to give away. We must be the force for good that this world so badly needs.

For many, driving across the Golden Gate Bridge is part of their everyday routine. One may see the car stopped in front of them and curse the traffic causing them to be late for work. One might cross the bridge in its entirety without realizing what they're a part of. They're too consumed by their thoughts of nagging worries or what has to be done tomorrow, and the next day, and the next year. But they don't realize that crossing the Golden Gate Bridge is the direct path to a better life. If only they'd look up in awe. We must find beauty in others and in all that we do, our day-to-day existence, most important of all. When we do, we'll realize just how beautiful we are ourselves.

THIS VIEW NEVER GETS OLD. I look out from the roof of Ramin, Pete, and Luke's San Francisco apartment. It's Sunday in North Beach and the boys are downstairs watching football. I look up from my journal and gaze from one end of San Francisco to the other, noting the landmarks that give the city character and charm. The view is as good as any in the world; I watch ships sailing around Alcatraz. What a fascinating concept, Alcatraz. A prison on an island in the middle of the bay.

The light tower still scans the grounds at night, although now it's a novelty, a part of history.

I stand up from the metal table and stretch my arms over my head, gazing from one side of the bay to the other. *Look around. Notice life. Appreciate wherever you are.* I scan the rest of the city. When I turn, the sunlight shines down on me and warms my skin all the way through. I watch the bustling Italian neighborhood of North Beach come alive.

The distinct neighborhoods of San Francisco make it a treasure map; discoveries lie around every corner. I find the distinctions of North Beach delightful: the red, green, and white flags hanging over the city streets add color, a sure path to beauty in a world that's often black and white. The spires of Saints Peter and Paul Church stand as a symbol of community and togetherness. Coit Tower sits on the top of the hill in the distance, a beacon like the lighthouse, a guide that tells me I'm home.

"Yo, Vince," Ramin's voice breaks me from my reverie. He is wearing the Christmas onesie he broke out during last night's failed attempt at constructing a gingerbread house.

"My man, how are we doing?" I ask. He stretches and takes in the nourishing rays.

"Couldn't be better, just checking on ya."

I love this guy. "Thanks, buddy; it's an unbelievable day. Are you going to chill up here?" I ask, expecting him to keep me company. He grits his teeth and shakes his head, pointing with two fingers down to the apartment.

"Football—just wanted to say hi."

Arrows of Youth

"Of course, I appreciate it, sir," I reply with a laugh. He slowly heads back downstairs, and I'm left with my thoughts. My heart is full of so much joy. I wish I could bottle up this feeling and break the bottle like a fire extinguisher whenever life becomes too much to bear. *I can.*

IN TWENTY YEARS, we'll remember the word *covid* and shudder at the thought—*2020, what a nightmare that was.* But is it? Yes, to the families affected beyond words from the loss of loved ones, it is. There's no way to reconcile the pain that so many human beings have had to endure. But that doesn't mean it can't get better. It'll take time to heal. While those that have passed have reached the end of their life on Earth, their deaths mustn't be in vain. There is a chance, if we allow it to be, for this to be a new beginning—*a modern Renaissance.*

As much as we've felt alone during this unprecedented period, we've come together as communities and as resilient individuals. The details of this year won't matter, not the individual days of loneliness or the moments of fear. What will matter is the feeling of togetherness, because together, we will overcome. The details of this trip won't matter, either. But perhaps I'll remember this moment forever: sitting on my best friend's roof in San Francisco after weeks of digging deep within myself. I'll remember how inspired I feel, like I can do anything, be anything, and achieve anything, *just by looking inward.* I'll remember feeling grateful for the people in my life, the people that matter more than any *thing* or *goal* could ever measure up to. I'll remember feeling grateful simply for the chance to be alive, as if for the first time.

I went on this road trip through California and the Pacific Northwest because I felt a calling to a part of the world that has always captivated me. I couldn't have expected this, an adventure that has profoundly enriched my mind, body, and soul. I've connected with people out in the world who continue to live from a place of love.

I've connected with friends I feel so lucky to have in my life. From the bottom of my heart, I believe that people in this world are good. Sometimes we mask our need to connect and we buy into the negativity that divides us. But when we get out there and talk, acknowledge, and support each other, when we foster curiosity, love, and remain open, we see people are truly good. Often all it takes is a smile to be a difference in somebody's life. An act of encouragement can make somebody realize what they're capable of. *An act of encouragement is the greatest gift that we can give.*

IN THIS PAST YEAR, we've been forced to take time to step back and assess what matters. I know that this is it. It's acting in a way that contributes to the binding light connecting us all. It's marveling at the sheer beauty, power, and peace of the natural world, forever and always, no matter where I am. My appreciation for our home, *this planet,* runs deep; it's so incredibly inspiring what's out there—the sights, the smells, the sounds—the life. Yet, we don't have to go anywhere to tap into the magic. We are meaning. We are love. We are unfathomable, beautiful beings. Sometimes it's best not to try to understand. *Sometimes it's best to just be.*

The church bell begins to ring. No matter who you are or what you're going through, the bell rings for you. If you're alone, just listen; think about the others who hear it too. Stop. Let yourself be swept away by the chiming bell, the sound that unites us all. I shut my journal, signaling the end of this journey, and the end of a year like no other.

DECEMBER 23rd. I returned to Malibu a couple of days ago. I often take this walk when I'm back home at my mom's, a quick jaunt around the neighborhood to look up at the night sky. I've seen Alfred a few times here since that fateful day in summer; he always has a fresh course for me to sink my teeth into. The winter air is chilly and revitalizing; it's a perfect Malibu night.

Earlier today, I went on a hike with my dad, Duke, and Jesse. To have a father and brothers who are my best friends is a blessing. We're friends across ages, from seventeen to sixty-four. I look up to my dad every single day as somebody who represents what matters in life. At least, that's how I see it.

My dad treasures his health, the one thing we can't pay for. He earns it day in and day out. He treasures his time on this Earth. That makes me want to give everything I have, and never take for granted what I've been given. A walk is the perfect way to appreciate what I have—my breath, my ability to see the clouds move, and my capacity to make a decision from my own volition. I make my way down to the beach and feel the sand beneath my feet. *Nothing can be as important as this.*

My parents and I, my friends and my brothers, all the humans of this Earth, we're growing together, right here and now. We're creating history. Together, and only together, will we create a history that is positive. We may come to see this time as a blessing. *I know I do.*

When I look up into the December sky, I notice a luminous ring around the moon. It looks like a halo, an angel looking down on us. *It wants us to keep going.*

This journey, this experience, this year is an *arrow of youth*. It will always be with me. This year is a collective arrow for us all. The future is uncertain; yet I couldn't be more encouraged to continue taking steps forward as a planet. We have an opportunity—what we can focus on right now and forevermore is our ability to appreciate this life for what it is—*a gift*. This belief becomes more vital every day I wake up and open my eyes.

Vincent

Dawn of Spring

The essence of hope is intrinsic;
Eyes open seconds fall Earth turns
And we turn too
But the body stops and stares in
Space, frozen, unable to move,
Paralyzed, gripped, unable to step
Beyond self-imposed reality;
Held down find it difficult to
Breathe, but then,
Freedom from reverie
Comes in words from someone close
Who wants the life they see
To breathe, who wants the
Life they see to bloom
Like flowers of the coming dawn
When life's reborn once motionless.
Awakened from the senseless night
When touched by rays
Of guiding light.

Our dawn has come to wake us up
And feel the warmth that

Knows no end
With self it's time to make
Amends to then be there
A caring friend who needs to feel the
Touch of light to see that
Their soul too
Burns bright—
Brighter than long lost
Vanished stars
A star means hope through
Empty nights.
The heat is felt and when it burns
A white hot color passed through
Words derived from a heart that
Was once touched too,
I hope they've found their
Way to you,
Together, we will make it through.

It's spring; can you feel it?
Pass along this call for hope,
Step outside, and breathe.

Poetry by

Vincent Russell Van Patten

We are all Poets.

Poetry is the universal language

In which the world speaks.

END NOTES

1 "Timeline: WHO's COVID-19 Response." *World Health Organization*. Accessed April 15, 2021. https://www.who.int/emergencies/diseases/novel-coronavirus-2019/interactive-timeline?gclid=Cj0KCQjwyN-DBhCDARIsAFOELTnxSG74OnueciZ5RPCkc-MbYJM_zVc2HuKoGYjT5fchWkNiXQsnMuL8aAm60EALw_wcB#!

2 McConaughey, Matthew. *Greenlights*. New York: Crown, 2020.

3 Lakoff, Sanford A. *Max Lerner: Pilgrim in the Promised Land.* Chicago: University of Chicago Press, 1998.

4 Lerner, Max. *America as a Civilization: Life and Thought in the United States Today.* New York: Simon and Schuster, 1957.

5 Tocqueville, Alexis de. *Democracy in America.* New York: Knopf, 1994.

6 Falk, Jeff. "Study: Living Abroad Leads to a Clearer Sense of Self." *Rice News. Office of Public Affairs,* March 20, 2018. http://news.rice.edu/2018/03/20/study-living-abroad-leads-to-a-clearer-sense-of-self/.

7 Newton, Isaac. *Philosophiae Naturalis Principia Mathematica ("Mathematical Principles of Natural Philosophy"),* London, 1687; Cambridge, 1713; London, 1726. (Pirated versions of the 1713 edition were also published in Amsterdam in 1714 and 1723.)

8 Kors, Professor Alan Charles. *The Birth of the Modern Mind: The Intellectual History of the 17th & 18th Centuries.* The Great Courses. Lecture, n.d. Accessed March 18, 2021.

9 Kant, Immanuel. Kant. *What Is Enlightenment.* 1784. Accessed February 16, 2021. http://www.columbia.edu/acis/ets/CCREAD/etscc/kant.html#note1.

10 Stevenson, Shawn. "Build Amazing Relationships, Set Bigger Goals & Create an Extraordinary Mind with Vishen Lakhiani." *The Model Health Show.* Accessed March 18, 2021. https://themodel-healthshow.com/vishen-lakhiani/.

11 Diener, Ed. *History of Happiness. Pursuit of Happiness.* Accessed March 18, 2021. https://www.pursuit-of-happiness.org/history-of-happiness/ed-diener/.

12 Marcus, Aubrey. "Masking the Real Health Crisis with Shawn Stevenson." *Aubreymarcus.com,* September 30, 2020. https://www.aubreymarcus.com/blogs/aubrey-marcus-podcast/masking-the-real-health-crisis-with-shawn-stevenson-amp-276.

13 Powers, Richard. *The Overstory*. London: Random House UK, 2018.

14 Paolini, Christopher. *Eragon*. New York: Alfred A. Knopf, 2003.

15 Michener, James A. *The World Is My Home: A Memoir*. New York: Dial Press, 2015.

16 Lakhiani, Vishen. *The Buddha and the Badass: The Secret Spiritual Art of Succeeding at Work*. New York: Rodale, 2020.

17 Michener, James A. *Tales of the South Pacific*. New York: Macmillan Co, 1968.

18 Harari, Yuval Noah. *Sapiens: A Brief History of Humankind*. London: Vintage, 2019.

19 Bryson, Bill. *A Short History of Nearly Everything*. London: Black Swan, 2016.

20 Ellis, Erle C. *Anthropocene: A Very Short Introduction.* Oxford: Oxford University Press, 2018.

21 Rume, Tanjena, and S.M. Didar-Ul Islam. *"Environmental Effects of COVID-19 Pandemic and Potential Strategies of Sustainability."* Heliyon. U.S. National Library of Medicine, September 2020. https://www.ncbi.nlm.nih.gov/pmc/articles/PMC7498239/.

22 Harari, Yuval Noah. *Homo Deus: A Brief History of Tomorrow*. London: Harper, 2018.

23 Iggulden, Conn. *Genghis: Birth of an Empire*. New York: Delacorte Press, 2007.

24 Lancel, Serge. *Hannibal*. Paris: Fayard, 1995.

25 Steinbeck, John. *East of Eden*. London: Penguin Books Ltd, 2017.

26 Scripture quotations taken from The Holy Bible, New International Version NIV. Copyright 1973, 1978, 1984, 2011 by Biblica, Inc. Used by permission. All rights reserved worldwide.

27 Benson, Jackson J. *John Steinbeck, Writer: A Biography*. New York: Penguin Books, 1990.

28 Peterson, Jordan B. *12 Rules for Life: An Antidote to Chaos*. Toronto, Canada: Random House Canada, 2018.

29 Ferriss, Tim. "Yuval Noah Harari on The Story of Sapiens, Forging the Skill of Awareness, and The Power of Disguised Books (#477)." *Tim.blog*, October 27, 2020. https://tim.blog/2020/10/27/yuval-noah-harari/.

30 Harari Yuval Noah. *21 Lessons for the 21st Century*. London: Vintage, 2019.

31 Williamson, Chris. "#286 - Dr Zach Bush MD - Why We Shouldn't Aim For A New Normal." *Chriswillx.com*, February 22, 2021.

32 Orwell, George. *1984*. New York: Signet Classic, 1961.

33 Youths, Gang of. *Do Not Let Your Spirit Wane*. Go Farther in Lightness. Mosy Recordings. 2018. Record.

34 Graham, Daniel W. "Heraclitus." *Stanford Encyclopedia of Philosophy*, September 3, 2019. Last modified September 3, 2019. Accessed March 5, 2021. https://plato.stanford.edu/entries/heraclitus/.

35 Whitman, Walt. "A Noiseless Patient Spider by Walt Whitman." *Poetry Foundation*. Accessed April 17, 2021. https://www.poetry-foundation.org/poems/45473/a-noiseless-patient-spider.

36 Stevenson, Shawn. "TMHS 447: Your Level of Exposure Determines Your Level of Success – With Guest Jemal King." *The Model Health Show*, December 8, 2020. https://themodelhealthshow.com/jemal-king-success/.

37 Pressfield, Steven. *The War of Art*. New York: Black Irish Entertainment, 2012.

38 Whitman, Walt. *Leaves of Grass: The First (1855) Edition*. New York: Penguin Books, 2005.

39 Morris, Roy. *The Better Angel: Walt Whitman in the Civil War*. New York: Oxford University Press, 2001.

40 Kerouac, Jack. *On the Road*. New York: Penguin Books, 2019.

41 Hemingway, E., interviewed by G. Plimpton. "The Art of Fiction No. 21." *The Paris Review*. Last modified February 20, 2020. Accessed March 6, 2021. https://www.theparisreview.org/interviews/4825/the-art-of-fiction-no-21-ernest-hemingway.

42 Popova, Maria. "How Cooking Civilized Us: Michael Pollan on Food as Social Glue and Anti-Corporate Activism." *Brain Pickings*. Last modified September 18, 2015. Accessed March 7, 2021. https://www.brainpickings.org/2013/04/24/michael-pollan-cooked/.

Arrows of Youth

[43] Verdolin, Dr. Jennifer. "The Upside of Eating Together." *Psychology Today*, November 29, 2019. Last modified November 29, 2019. Accessed March 7, 2021. https://www.psychologytoday.com/us/blog/wild-connections/201911/the-upside-eating-together.

[44] Isaacson, Walter. *Leonardo Da Vinci*. New York: Simon & Schuster Paperbacks, 2018.

[45] Lakhiani, Vishen. *The Buddha and the Badass: The Secret Spiritual Art of Succeeding at Work*. New York: Rodale, 2020.

[46] Hatfield, Gary, "René Descartes." The Stanford Encyclopedia of Philosophy (Summer 2018 Edition), Edward N. Zalta (ed.), URL = <https://plato.stanford.edu/archives/sum2018/entries/descartes/>

[47] Sadhguru. *Inner Engineering: A Yogi's Guide to Joy*. New York: Spiegel & Grau, 2016.

[48] Thoreau, Henry David. *Walden*. S.l.: Arcturus, 2020.

[49] Manson, Mark. *The Subtle Art of Not Giving a F*ck: A Counterintuitive Approach to Living a Good Life*. New York: HarperLuxe, 2019.

[50] Clavell, James. *Shogun*. New York: Random House, 1975.

[51] Scripture quotations taken from The Holy Bible, New International Version NIV. Copyright 1973, 1978, 1984, 2011 by Biblica, Inc. Used by permission. All rights reserved worldwide.

[52] Rabin, Sheila, "Nicolaus Copernicus." *The Stanford Encyclopedia of Philosophy* (Fall 2019 Edition), Edward N. Zalta (ed.), URL = <https://plato.stanford.edu/archives/fall2019/entries/copernicus/>.

53 Panek, Richard. "The Year of Albert Einstein." Smithsonian Magazine, June 2005. Accessed 2021. https://www.smithsonianmag.com/science-nature/the-year-of-albert-einstein-75841381/.

54 Thomas, Dylan. "Do Not Go Gentle into That Good Night by Dylan Thomas - Poems | Academy of American Poets." Poets.org. Academy of American Poets. Accessed April 17, 2021. https://poets.org/poem/do-not-go-gentle-good-night.

55 Knausgaard, Karl Ove. *My Struggle: Book Six*. Brooklyn, NY: Archipelago Books, 2018.

56 Tolstoy, Leo. *War and Peace*. London: Vintage Classics, 2008.

57 Zweig, Stefan, and Anthea Bell. *The World of Yesterday*. London: Pushkin Press, 2014.

58 Carlin, Dan. *Hardcore History 60 – The Celtic Holocaust*. Dan Carlin, August 2017. https://www.dancarlin.com/product/hardcore-history-60-the-celtic-holocaust/.

59 Roochnik, Professor David. *Introduction to Greek Philosophy*. The Great Courses. Lecture, n.d. Accessed March 18, 2021.

60 Foxes, Fleet. *The Shrine*. Helplessness Blues. Bella Union, 2011. Record.

61 "Deep Ties Between Sister Cities of Otsuchi, Japan and Fort Bragg, Cali." *PRWeb*, March 16, 2011. https://www.prweb.com/releases/2011/03/prweb5163054.htm.

62 Shetty, Jay. *Think Like a Monk: Train Your Mind for Peace and Purpose Every Day*. New York: Simon & Schuster, 2020.

Arrows of Youth

[63] Zweig, Stefan. *Montaigne.* London: Pushkin Press, 2015.

[64] Montaigne, Michel de, and Donald M. Frame. *The Complete Essays of Montaigne.* Stanford, CA: Stanford University Press, 2002.

[65] Frost, Robert. "The Road Not Taken." Poetry Foundation. Accessed March 25, 2021. https://www.poetryfoundation.org/poems/44272/the-road-not-taken.

[66] Peterson, Jordan B. *Beyond Order: 12 More Rules for Life.* New York: Random House Large Print, 2021.

[67] Peterson, Jordan. *Biblical Series II: Genesis 1: Chaos & Order Transcript.* Last modified April 17, 2018. Accessed February 14, 2021. https://www.jordanbpeterson.com/transcripts/biblical-series-ii/.

Arrows of Youth

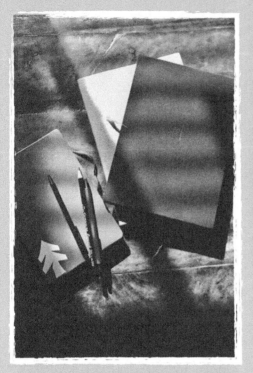

VINCENT'S COMMONPLACE BOOKS; TOKYO, JAPAN;
PARIS, FRANCE: OLYMPIC NATIONAL PARK, WASHINGTON

VINCENT RUSSELL VAN PATTEN is a writer, media creator, and co-host of *The Dare to Dream Podcast*. Most importantly, he's an inspired citizen of our ever-changing world. Vincent fosters a profound passion for travel, history, spirituality, personal growth, and authentic human connection. His heart yearns to explore the natural world, the cities, towns, and everything else which we call home.

When Vincent was young, his favorite shows were on the *Travel Channel*. Andrew Zimmern, Adam Richman, and Anthony Bourdain were his guys! Vincent never tired of watching Zimmern eat bugs, or Richman devour a sixty-two-ounce steak in less than an hour.

Yet, it was Bourdain who inspired Vincent to journey into the unknown. Bourdain's *No Reservations & Parts Unknown* made him believe that it's an art form to uncover a city's essence. The solution is simple: do as the locals do, slow down, walk, ask questions, observe, *live*. This often means staying in one place, watching the day go by, and simply being present. Vincent wouldn't be who he is without Bourdain's influence.

His life has emboldened Vincent to be a curious explorer of this progressive planet. Vincent hopes to honor Bourdain by following his dream of traveling the world with a full heart, and sharing what he learns on every step of the journey. He strives to be grateful for every day, every second, and every experience of this gift we call life.

Through his projects, Vincent dreams of instilling others with the same enthusiasm and sheer joy he felt when crafting his latest arrow in the mountains of Yosemite, the towering trees of Northern California, and the jaw-dropping scenery of the Pacific Northwest.

vincentvanpatten.com

Instagram: @vincentvanpatten   Medium: @vincentvanpatten

Twitter: @vincevanpatten   Facebook.com/vincentvanpattenwriter

Made in the USA
Coppell, TX
25 June 2021